Twayne's English Authors Series

Sylvia E. Bowman, *Editor*

INDIANA UNIVERSITY

Aphra Behn

63

APHRA BEHN

by

FREDERICK M. LINK

A survey of the works of Aphra Behn, "the incomparable Astrea," an interesting and prolific writer whose career spanned the middle decades of the Restoration period. She was probably the first woman to make her living by her pen, and she competed articulately and successfully for a place amongst the better writers of Restoration comedies. Her plays were popular and some of them were still being staged well into the eighteenth century. Yet the attacks of the moralists upon her supposedly profligate life and indecent writings have condemned her to relative obscurity, and the only substantial edition of her works has been out of print for nearly half a century.

This study encompasses her plays, poems, translations, and stories, and included, for the reader unfamiliar with Mrs. Behn, brief plot summaries of the plays and the short novels. Professor Link stresses Aphra Behn's achievements, especially as a dramatist, but approaches his subject in a realistic way, and does not advance her as an undiscovered genius.

Aphra Behn

By **FREDERICK M. LINK**

University of Nebraska

Twayne Publishers, Inc. :: New York

For

Harry and Kathleen Link

ABOUT THE AUTHOR

Frederick M. Link has studied at Southwestern-at-Memphis and at Boston University, where he received his M.A. and his Ph.D. He has taught at Boston University and is currently Associate Professor of English at the University of Nebraska. Professor Link's research has centered upon Restoration and eighteenth-century literature and the English novel. Among his publications are an edition of Sir Walter Scott's *Fortunes of Nigel,* with introduction, notes, and glossary, and an edition of Aphra Behn's *The Rover* for the Regent's Restoration Drama Series.

Preface

Most of what has been written about Aphra Behn's life is based on conjecture and misinformation. For example, after three hundred years we do not yet know her maiden name, the date of her birth, or the circumstances surrounding her trip to Surinam and her marriage. The two main contemporary sources are the "History of the Life and Memoirs of Mrs. Behn," which forms the preface to the 1696 edition of her *Histories and Novels*, and the rather similar but abbreviated "Account of the Life of the Incomparable Mrs. Behn" which prefaces *The Younger Brother* (1696). Both of these prefaces, probably the work of Charles Gildon, contain much obviously fictitious material, as well as some information which scholars have been unable to corroborate. Mrs. Behn herself gives very little information beyond asserting she had spent some time in Surinam, and her contemporaries were far more interested in her character than in the details of her life.

Nor has there been much criticism of her work. Only two books, both fairly recent, have been devoted to the subject, and only that by George Woodcock (1948) is of real value. The same situation exists with reference to shorter essays; aside from one article on her use of setting, and brief discussions of *Oronooko*, no significant critical study of any aspect of her work has appeared in print.

This book is a survey of Mrs. Behn's plays, poems, translations, and novels. Since her plays are her most important body of work, they have received most attention. Chapter Two considers the three apprentice dramas of the early 1670's. The period between 1676 and 1682 is treated more fully, not only because she was more productive, but because all her best comedies were written within this seven-year span. The two late plays, the two produced after her death, and the four often attributed to her are discussed in Chapter Four. Since Mrs. Behn, like most other dramatists of her day, borrowed from and adapted earlier plays, a chapter on her sources and her use of them concludes this section of the book.

The last half of the book is devoted to her non-dramatic work. Her poetry, including prologues and epilogues, songs, and panegyrics, is the subject of Chapter Six. The translations, primarily from the French, are considered separately. Chapter Eight takes up *Oronooko* and her other short fictions. Chapter One is an introduction to Mrs. Behn's life and times, and Chapter Nine a summary and evaluation of her career and reputation.

Throughout, I have directed myself to the general reader rather than to the specialist in Restoration literature, keeping in mind both the wide audience addressed by Twayne's English Authors Series and the difficulty of access to Mrs. Behn's works. Since the last collected edition, edited by Montague Summers in 1915, has long been out of print, and since her work is rarely anthologized, I have quoted liberally throughout, not only to support my discussion but as well to illustrate the wide range of her achievement. All references, except where indicated, are to first editions. All dates are New Style, to conform to the modern calendar. Spelling (except of proper names), punctuation, and capitalization have throughout been brought into accord with modern practice. The italic type commonly used in Restoration prefaces, prologues, and so on, has been replaced by roman. Quotations from the plays have been set up in the format used successfully by the Regents Restoration Drama Series, and I have occasionally altered the lineation of the quarto texts. The result, it is hoped, will be clear and readable, and certainly more accurate than Summers' text, which is eclectic and largely based on derivative editions.

I wish here to thank the staff of the Houghton Library of Harvard University for its courtesy and helpfulness over a period of several months. Officials of the Yale, Newberry, Huntington, Folger, Clark, and University of Texas libraries provided me with useful bibliographical information. I am indebted to the Research Council of the University of Nebraska for a fellowship in support of the book, and to my wife, to Dr.

and Mrs. Haskel Cohen, and to Professors Michael Alssid, and the late David Bonnell Green for their assistance and encouragement.

FREDERICK M. LINK

University of Nebraska

Contents

Preface   7

Chronology   13

1. The Life and Times of Aphra Behn   17

2. The Dramatist: Early Plays   29

3. The Dramatist: Mid-Career   41

4. The Dramatist: Late, Posthumous, and Doubtful plays   74

5. The Dramatist: Sources   91

6. The Poet   102

7. The Translator   116

8. The Novelist   130

9. Summing Up: Aphra Behn, 1689-1967   152

Notes and References   159

Selected Bibliography   171

Index   179

Chronology

NOTE: *The date of first publication of a play is given at the end of its entry.*

ca. 1640   Aphra Behn born; maiden name, place and date of birth, and parentage unknown.

1663   *ca.* November—*ca.* February, 1664, probable residence in Surinam during this period.

ca. 1664   May have married an English merchant of Dutch ancestry named Behn.

ca. 1665   Death of Mr. Behn?

1666   July, to Antwerp as a spy for the crown. Return to England, probably between December, 1666 and May, 1667.

1668   Brief imprisonment for debt.

1670   September, *The Forced Marriage*, tragicomedy, produced at Lincoln's Inn Fields; 1671.

1671   February, *The Amorous Prince*, tragicomedy, Lincoln's Inn Fields; 1671.

1673   February, *The Dutch Lover*, comedy, Dorset Garden; 1673.

1676   July, *Abdelazer*, tragedy, Dorset Garden; 1677. *ca.* September, *The Town Fop*, comedy, Dorset Garden; 1677.

1677   February, *The Debauchee*, comedy, possibly by Mrs. Behn; 1677. March, *The Rover*, comedy, Dorset Garden; 1677. *ca.* September, *The Counterfeit Bridegroom*, comedy, possibly by Mrs. Behn; 1677.

1678   January, *Sir Patient Fancy*, comedy, Dorset Garden; 1678.

1679   *ca.* March, *The Feigned Courtesans*, comedy, Dorset Garden; 1679. *ca.* September, *The Young King*, tragicomedy, Dorset Garden; 1683.

1680   *ca.* June, *The Revenge*, comedy, possibly by Mrs. Behn; 1680.

1681 *ca.* January, *The Second Part of the Rover,* comedy; Dorset Garden; 1681. November, *The False Count,* comedy-farce, Dorset Garden; 1682. *ca.* December, *The Roundheads,* political comedy, Dorset Garden; 1682.

1682 *ca.* March, *Like Father, Like Son,* comedy, Dorset Garden; never printed. *ca.* May, *The City Heiress,* comedy, Dorset Garden; 1682. August, arrested for attack on Monmouth in epilogue to *Romulus and Hersilia.*

1684 *Poems upon Several Occasions; Love Letters between a Nobleman and His Sister,* fiction.

1685 February, death of Charles II and accession of James II. *A Pindaric on the Death of Our Late Sovereign; A Poem . . . to . . . Catherine Queen Dowager; A Pindaric Poem on the Happy Coronation; Miscellany,* edited by and including poems of Mrs. Behn.

1686 April, *The Lucky Chance,* comedy, Theatre Royal, Drury Lane; 1687. *La Montre; or, The Lover's Watch,* translation from Bonnecorse.

1687 March, *The Emperor of the Moon,* comedy-farce, Dorset Garden; 1687. *To . . . Christopher Duke of Albemarle; To the Memory of . . . George Duke of Buckingham;* verses for Francis Barlow's edition of Aesop; *The Amours of Philander and Sylvia* (Part III of *Love Letters*).

1688 *A Congratulatory Poem to Her Most Sacred Majesty; The Fair Jilt,* fiction; *A Congratulatory Poem . . . on the Happy Birth of the Prince of Wales; Oronooko,* fiction; *Agnes de Castro,* adaptation of French story by Mlle de Brillac; *The History of Oracles,* translation from the French of Fontenelle; *Lycidus,* translation of Paul Tallemant's fantasy; *A Poem to Sir Roger L'Estrange; To Poet Bavius,* an attack on a John Baber poem.

1689 *A Congratulatory Poem to . . . Queen Mary; The History of the Nun,* fiction; *The Lucky Mistake,* fiction; "Of Plants," translation of Book VI of Cowley's *Sex libri plantarum; A Pindaric Poem to the Reverend Dr. Burnet.* April 16, death of Aphra Behn; burial in Westminster Abbey. November, *The Widow Ranter,* comedy, Drury Lane; 1690.

1696   February, *The Younger Brother,* comedy, Drury Lane; 1696.

1698   "The Adventure of the Black Lady"; "The Court of the King of Bantam"; "The Nun, or Perjured Beauty"; *The Unfortunate Happy Lady; The Unfortunate Bride; The Wandering Beauty;* all fiction.

1700   *The Dumb Virgin; The Unhappy Mistake;* both fiction.

CHAPTER 1

The Life and Times of Aphra Behn

ASIDE from the brief preface to the first quarto of *The Younger Brother* (1696), the earliest information about Aphra Behn's birth and parentage comes in the "Memoirs on the Life of Mrs. Behn by a Gentlewoman of her Acquaintance," which introduces the first edition of the collected *Histories and Novels*. Charles Gildon, who wrote the first notice, is also the probable author of this one; it appeared later the same year, and he was not above masquerading as a woman if he felt it to his advantage. He pretends to know his subject well, but some of what he says can be derived from Mrs. Behn's published works; and much more, as W. J. Cameron has pointed out,[1] seems embroidered from literary fragments coming into Gildon's hands as one of her executors. However, the author of the "Memoirs" does say that "she was a gentlewoman by birth, of a good family in the city of Canterbury in Kent; her father's name was Johnson, whose relation to Lord Willoughby drew him, for the advantageous post of lieutenant-general of many isles, besides the continent of Surinam, from his quiet retreat at Canterbury . . ." ([A7ᵛ]).

This account was repeated in Gildon's revision of Gerard Langbaine's *The Lives and Characters of the English Dramatic Poets* (1699). He adds one detail: Mrs. Behn was herself born in Canterbury. So matters stood until September 5, 1884, when Edmund Gosse published his discovery of a marginal note in a manuscript copy of the Countess of Winchilsea's poems. Opposite a line of poetry referring to Mrs. Behn, the countess had written: "Mrs. Behn was daughter to a barber, who lived formerly in Wye, a little market town . . . in Kent. Though the account of her life before her works pretends otherwise, some persons now alive do testify upon their knowledge that to be her original." Gosse, inquiring of the vicar at Wye, was given that clergyman's reading of the parish register: "On July 10th, 1640, were baptized at Wye, Ayfara the daughter and Peter the son of John and Amy Johnson."[2] The new information was recorded for posterity in Gosse's article on Mrs. Behn for the *Dictionary of National Biography:* "She was the daughter of John Johnson, a barber."

The story was far from over, however. Montague Summers, preparing his edition of Mrs. Behn's works, had the vicar's entry checked. His informant found a major error: her name was not Johnson after all, but "Ayfara, or Aphara (Aphra) Amis or Amies, the daughter of John and Amy Amis or Amies."[3] There was no mention of her father's occupation: "There is no such thing as a quality, trade, and profession column in the register."[4] Now it was John Amis who must have gone to Surinam, and who was related to Lord Willoughby. Or John Amis was somehow connected with a Johnson who was related to Lord Willoughby. Walter and Clare Jerrold discovered a John Johnson in the *Calendar of State Papers,* Colonial Series 1661-68, and connected him tenuously with Lord Willoughby,[5] but they were unable to connect him directly with Mrs. Behn.

Both of the general books on Aphra Behn, Victoria Sackville-West's *Aphra Behn* (1928) and George Woodcock's *The Incomparable Aphra* (1948), give accounts of the above material, and it is still reflected in the card catalogues of major libraries: "Behn, Aphra (Amis), 1640-1689." But an Englishman named A. Purvis, happening to check further at Wye, found that Summers had not gone far enough either; he had forgotten the burial register. In January, 1954, Purvis printed the relevant entry: "1640, Afara ye daughter of John Amis, July ye 12th: Peter ye son of John Amis, July ye 16th."[6] Extensive searches by P. D. Mundy[7] and others have failed to add anything new. After more than three hundred years and three different sets of "facts," no one knows when or where Mrs. Behn was born, or who her parents were.

Nor is anything known of her early childhood. The "Memoirs" say that her father, on his voyage to the West Indies, took with him "his wife and children; and in that number Afra . . . who even in the first bud of infancy, discovered such early hopes of her riper years, that she was equally her parents' joy and fears . . ." ([A7ᵛ]). This suggests that Aphra was a young child, but shortly after in the account she is said to have left behind her the broken hearts of lovers, "that sighed to possess what was scarce yet arrived to a capacity of easing their pain, if she had been willing . . ." ([A8]). If this suspiciously conventional phrasing can be trusted, she was in early adolescence. At any rate, "Her father lived not to see that land . . . which she so admirably describes in *Oronooko*: where you may also find what adventures happened to her in that country [Surinam]. . . . The lord, her father's friend, that was not then arrived, perished in a hurricane . . . [She] only waited the arrival of the next ships to convey her back to her desired England; where she soon after . . . arrived . . ." ([A8ᵛ], [b1ᵛ]).

Oronooko (1688), contains a number of details which corroborate the "Memoirs." Mrs. Behn says that she was "an eyewitness to a great part" of the story (p. 2), but that her "stay was to be short in that country, because my father died at sea, and never arrived to possess the honor that was designed him . . .; so that . . . we were obliged to continue on our voyage . . ." (p. 148). There are references to her mother and sister (p. 238), to her stay at St. John's Hill (p. 152), and to known persons in Surinam like John Trefry (p. 102), Colonel Martin (pp. 209-10), and Deputy Governor Byam (p. 196). The chronology she gives is rather confused, but it is nearly impossible to believe that the biographical material in the story is mere fabrication on her part.

Ernest Bernbaum, however, believed just that. In a paper published in 1913,[8] he argued that her story comes from George Warren's *Impartial Description of Surinam* (1667), and that the biographical details were added for "realistic" effect. His argument is only superficially convincing, and has been effectively answered by H. D. Benjamins, Harrison Platt, and W. J. Cameron.[9] Cameron's summary is authoritative: "Until someone *proves* that one of Aphra Behn's autobiographical comments (apart from the formal eye-witness claims and the incidents forming part of her plots) are untrue, I believe they should be taken as more authoritative than any posthumous biographer's statements. As far as the Surinam episode is concerned, it may be said that external contemporary evidence does not conclusively establish the truth of this principle, but it is not incompatible with it."[10] He suggests that Mrs. Behn probably arrived in Surinam "towards the end of 1663," and that she left "before the beginning of March 1664" (p. 10). The circumstantial evidence for both dates is quite strong.

Little or nothing is known about her life in Surinam beyond what she tells us in *Oronooko*. Harrison Platt, trying to account for the government's choice of her as an agent in Holland and for the attack on Byam (like herself a Tory) in the novel, argues that she "went out to Surinam with William Scot, son of the regicide Thomas Scot, a political radical and at best a dubious character."[11] He relates her attack on Byam to her association with Scot, and their departure to his imminent arrest for debt; reversing the usual account, he argues that they went directly to Holland, and that she came to England to negotiate his pardon sometime after April, 1666. Employed by the crown to use her contact to spy on the disaffected English group in Holland, her affection for Scot caused her to send little information and to push for his pardon. According to Platt, when she realized she could do nothing, she returned to England.

As a letter from Byam to Sir Robert Harley in March, 1664, suggests,[12] Scot (the Celadon of the letter) was probably in Surinam at the time; if so, he almost certainly knew Mrs. Behn (the letter's Astrea). But it is most unlikely that they returned to Europe together, or that Mrs. Behn was in Holland prior to her mission for the crown. And, while Platt's hypothesis does account for the government's choice of Aphra Behn as its agent, there is no reason to assume that she was Scot's mistress, or took the job to serve his interest. In fact, the extant documents in the Public Record Office suggest that she did her best to secure useful information for her superiors.

At any rate, the first unquestioned facts in Mrs. Behn's life concern this mission to Antwerp. Nineteen documents survive among the official State Papers; Cameron prints them in full and provides a full discussion of their relevance.[13] They cover the period from July 27 through December 26, 1666, and detail her activities in seeking information about English malcontents and about Dutch plans against England. Some of her information was valuable;[14] but, despite her piteous appeals for funds, there is little reason to quarrel with Cameron's judgment that, considering Charles II's finances at the time, the £125 or so she was paid was not inadequate.[15] When her work proved fruitless, she returned to England at her own expense; as three petitions apparently written toward the end of 1668 imply,[16] she borrowed the necessary funds. Unable to pay the money back, she was imprisoned for debt on the order of one Butler. Lord Arlington, under whose authority she had worked, may have had her released; Thomas Killigrew, who appears to have suggested her appointment, is another possibility.[17]

At some point between her return from Surinam in 1664 and her brief career as a spy in 1666, she probably married a man named Behn, possibly a merchant of Dutch extraction. Emily Hahn, in *Purple Passage,* suggests that she met him in Surinam; but there is no supporting evidence—and the Dutch did not take over the country until after Mrs. Behn's departure. Bernbaum doubted the marriage, but it is not likely, as Woodcock points out (p. 28), that she would invent such a name for herself and use it in official correspondence. Hargreaves has suggested a candidate,[18] but has not been able to tie him directly to Mrs. Behn. No record of the marriage is known to exist, but in an age of lampoon and innuendo, there is little contemporary suggestion that it was a fiction. Whatever the circumstances, it is likely that Mr. Behn, whoever he was, died very shortly after the marriage: her letters from Antwerp do not mention him, nor do her 1668 petitions. Mrs. Behn herself never once refers to him in a long and varied career. The best guess is that he died about 1665 or 1666, possibly of the plague.

Aphra Behn's decision to attempt the fiercely competitive theatrical world was unusual. In our own day it is uncommon; in hers, it was unprecedented. A few women before her time had dabbled more or less seriously in literature—Katherine Philips, for example. But Mrs. Behn was the first of them to depend on her talents and industry for her bread. A few years earlier, she might not have survived. But by 1670 London was recovering rapidly from the ravages of the plague and the Great Fire, and the novelty of her position as a female playwright might even have been appreciated. The two dramatic compa-

nies—the King's Men and the Duke's Men—were strong, and the
two theaters were presenting new plays as well as reviving Jacobean and Renaissance favorites. Her association with the Duke's
company is curious, since Thomas Killigrew was connected with
the other and his is the name appearing in connection with her
experiences in Antwerp. Perhaps, as Woodcock suggests (p.
49), her choice owes something to Davenant's introduction of
women actresses to replace the boys who took such roles before
the Restoration.

She seems to have known a number of people associated with
the theater before 1670. The story of her kindness to young
Thomas Otway in letting him have a part in *The Forced Marriage* with disastrous results is well known, and retailed in the
reminiscences of the prompter John Downes.[19] It is likely that
she had at least met many of the dramatists of the period: Sir
George Etherege, William Wycherley, John Dryden, Elkanah
Settle, Nathaniel Lee, Edward Ravenscroft, Thomas Shadwell,
Edward Howard, and others. She probably knew a number of
the actors, perhaps the Bettertons, who led the troupe at the
Duke's Theatre. But no one knows how she got her entry, or
how she learned the elements of her craft. Her knowledge of
details of staging, for example, apparent even in *The Forced
Marriage,* suggests either a period of apprenticeship or careful
observation of performances over an extended period of time.
But almost nothing is known of her at this time, except what one
can conjecture from the plays themselves and from their prefaces, prologues, and epilogues.

The Forced Marriage did well enough to encourage her, and
The Amorous Prince soon followed. Her third play, *The Dutch
Lover,* did not meet with any success, though she defended it
in a long introduction to the published version. Though she
thought the actors had ruined the play, she attacked the critics,
who, she felt, had objected only because of her sex. Her defense
had to be made again and again in her career; the Grub Street
hacks apparently resented a woman's presence in their world,
and never ceased criticizing her works and her morals. In fact,
the attack was usually on both: they implied she was a strum-
pet, and called her works lascivious. Thus she had to defend
her plays against the charge of indecency, not because they

[22]

were any more indecent than other comedies of the period, but because women were not supposed to write bawdy on equal terms with men.

The preface to *The Dutch Lover* is echoed fourteen years later in that to *The Lucky Chance:*

But I make a challenge to any person of common sense and reason ... to read any of my comedies and compare 'em with others of this age, and if they find one word that can offend the chastest ear, I will submit to all their peevish cavils. But right or wrong, they must be criminal because a woman's ...

All I ask is the privilege for my masculine part the poet in me ... to tread in those successful paths my predecessors have so long thrived in, to take those measures that both the ancient and modern writers have set me, and by which they have pleased the world so well. If I must not, because of my sex, have this freedom . . . , I lay down my quill, . . . for I am not content to write for a third day only. I value fame as much as if I had been born a hero; and if you rob me of that, I can retire from the ungrateful world, and scorn its fickle favors.   ([A3ᵛ]; al)

The failure of her third play seems to have kept her from the stage for more than three years. Nothing is known of her from February, 1673, until *Abdelazer* was produced, probably in July, 1676. Her circle of acquaintance certainly grew, but we have no details. George Woodcock, surveying her relationship to the literary and non-literary worlds of her day, shows that she was widely admired both for wit and beauty. She knew poets and patrons like Lord Lansdowne; playwrights like Dryden, Otway, and Ravenscroft; lawyers like John Hoyle; students like Thomas Creech, the translator; doctors; actors and actresses; musicians; painters. She wrote lyrics and panegyrics to some of them, and was often the subject of commendatory verses by them. She was considered by the scandalmongers a Venus of easy virtue, or worse, but the maliciousness of Tom Brown's account[20] must be balanced against the strength and independence evident throughout her works, and against the known reputation of Tom Brown himself.

When she returned to the stage, she began a period of feverish activity: within two years she had seen her one tragedy, and three of her best comedies (*The Town Fop, The Rover*, and *Sir Patient Fancy*) produced at the Dorset Garden Theatre; it is possible that she did at least two adaptations in addition. In the spring of 1679 came *The Feigned Courtesans*, a good comedy of intrigue, followed that fall by *The Young King*, a tragicomedy begun much earlier ˉand unsuccessfully reworked. Between January, 1681, and the spring of 1682 no less than five of her plays were on the boards, including a fine comedy (*The City Heiress*) and an excellent farce (*The False Count*). Obviously, such a pace could not have been maintained had she not made use of plot materials from earlier plays; and, indeed, several of these plays are adaptations of French or English originals. Despite her many borrowings, and despite such bad plays as *The Young King* and *The Roundheads*, there is no doubt that she deserved her success. Her best comedies, as good as those of anyone in the period except Etherege, Congreve, and Wycherly, deserve to be better known.

That Mrs. Behn was an ardent Tory is evident from even a casual glance at her work. *The Rover* is obviously written from a Cavalier point of view, and is full of praise for Charles; and the prologue to *The Young King* ends with the hope that Heaven will "bless the King that keeps the land in peace." Her political alignment, in fact, is evident in her very first plays: both *The Forced Marriage* and *The Amorous Prince* include among their themes that divinity doth indeed hedge a king. Her loyalty to the Stuarts probably dates from her early life, reinforced by her brief career as a spy for Charles and by whatever patronage was given her plays by the monarch and his brother. The intensity of her convictions may be measured by the dedication of *The Second Part of the Rover* to James, then Duke of York, who was unpopular even among many Tories for the inflexibility of his Roman Catholic views. The language is the customary egregious flattery, but the tone and matter are those of a strong partisan.

As a Tory personally loyal to the Stuarts, Mrs. Behn must have resented the gradual rise of the Whigs after the Restoration. By the late 1670's they were a powerful force in English politics, and Tory writers, led by Dryden, made an increasing number of attacks on the party and on such prominent leaders as Buckingham, Monmouth, and Shaftesbury. In the fall of 1678, the so-called Popish Plot, fabricated by the vicious Titus Oates to establish the Whigs by associating the Tories with regicide and treason, forced national attention even more strongly on party differences. James was forced briefly into exile, and only shrewd maneuvering by Charles and the revelation of Oates's lies stemmed the tide of popular feeling and revived the Tories. Their first major step was to charge Shaftesbury with treasonable plotting against Charles. When the grand jury, dominated by Whigs, refused to indict him, returning a bill of *Ignoramus* in November, 1681, Tory fury knew no bounds. Tom D'Urfey's *Sir Barnaby Whig* had already appeared in September; Dryden's *Absalom and Achitophel* preceded the verdict by a fortnight; Otway contributed *Venice Preserved*, the other great work born out of the struggle, in February. In November, 1682, came Dryden and Lee's *Duke of Guise*, and in January, 1683, Crowne's *City Politics*.

The dedication to Part Two of *The Rover*, and of course the sentiments of the play itself, signaled Mrs. Behn's entry into the fray. Then in the fine prologue to *The False Count*, she appears ironically as a convert to the Whig cause:

> Know all ye Whigs and Tories of the pit
> (Ye furious Guelphs and Ghibelines of wit,
> Who for the cause and crimes of Forty-One
> So furiously maintain the quarrel on),
> Our author, as you'll find it writ in story,
> Has hitherto been a most wicked Tory;
> But now, to th' joy o'th' brethren be it spoken,
> Our sister's vain mistaking eyes are open;
> And wisely valuing her dear interest now,
> All-powerful Whigs, converted is to you. . . .
>
> Your conventicling miracles outdo
> All that the whore of Babylon e'er knew:
> By wondrous art you make rogues honest men,
> And when you please, transform 'em rogues again.
> Today a saint, if he but hang a papist,
> Preach a true protestant, your saint's turned atheist;
> And dying sacraments do less prevail,
> Than living ones, though took in lamb's-wool-ale.

Who would not then be for a commonweal,
To have the villain covered with his zeal? . . .

But should the Tories now, who will desert me,
Because they find no dry bobs on your party,
Resolve to hiss, as late did popish crew;
By yea and nay, she'll throw herself on you,
The grand inquest of Whigs, to whom she's true.
Then let 'em rail and hiss, and damn their fill,
Your verdict will be *Ignoramus* still.

The Roundheads (December, 1681) was a bulkier, if not a better, contribution to the Tory cause. The play satirizes the Whigs by recalling the last hours of the Commonwealth, and associating (at least by common inference) modern Whig politics with the power struggles between Lambert, Fleetwood, and the Committee of Safety. The play—dedicated to the Duke of Grafton, a natural son of Charles II—mixes adulation of the Duke with strong Tory sauce; and, presenting the play as a "small mirror of the late wretched times," the playwright appeals to Grafton to protect it against the venom of the Whigs. Praise of "The glorious martyr" and of Charles II alternates with a warning to the "royal lovely youth" to "beware of false ambition," a warning obviously striking not so much at Grafton as at Monmouth.

The attack continues in *The City Heiress*. Sir Timothy is manifestly Shaftesbury: his Whig views, his feasting of his supporters, his political intrigues, and his avarice are tellingly presented at many points in the play. Specific satiric reference is made to his support of the Exclusion Bill, to the *Ignoramus* verdict, and especially to his ambition to be elected king of Poland in 1675. The Tory sentiments of the play extended to its trappings; for Thomas Otway, who furnished the prologue, hits at the Puritans, at Titus Oates, and at the failure of a projected Whig dinner in April of 1682. The dedication to Henry Howard, then Earl of Arundel, commends the Howards for loyalty to the Crown. The author, who calls her work "in every part true Tory! Loyal all over, except one knave," thinks its favorable reception proves "honesty begins to come in fashion again, when loyalty is approved, and Whiggism becomes a jest where'er 'tis met with."

What further political plays Mrs. Behn might have produced is a matter for conjecture, for in August, 1682, she went too far in her satiric attacks on the Whigs. To the production of the anonymous *Romulus and Hersilia* she contributed a very biting prologue and epilogue, making in the latter a fairly obvious attack on Monmouth. Charles's affection for his natural son was erratic, but a personal attack usually meant his displeasure, and a warrant was issued on August 12 for the arrest of Mrs. Behn and the actress who spoke the epilogue (Lady Slingsby), on grounds they had made "abusive reflections upon persons of quality."[21] Nothing much came of the incident for the actress, who appeared in *The Duke of Guise* that winter; but it put an end to Mrs. Behn's political career so far as the stage was concerned. Her expression of her royalist sentiments must be followed from this point in her occasional poems on state occasions. As the discussion of these works in Chapter Six shows, her feelings did not change; if anything, they became stronger as the fortunes of the Stuarts waned and her own death approached. John Dryden's loyalty to his adopted faith was no stronger than hers to Charles and then to James.

She produced no more plays until the spring of 1686. The four-year gap in her dramatic career is an important one, not merely because of its length, but because Charles II died during it—in February, 1685. And though she remained intensely loyal to James II, she must have foreseen the danger to Stuart's hopes in his stubborn pursuit of the Catholic cause in England. She had published a major collection of her poems in 1684, and a long piece of epistolary fiction; thereafter, her work becomes increasingly miscellaneous in character, and references to poverty and illness occur frequently. Woodcock prints a letter to Tonson, written about 1684, in which she begs for £5 more for her *Poems*, and another from August, 1685, in which she binds herself to pay a £6 debt before two months are out.[22] Her last plays were *The Lucky Chance* (1686) and *The Emperor of the Moon* (1687). The other late works include most of her translations—of La Rochenfoucauld, Bonnecorse, Fontenelle, Tallemant, and Cowley—all of her fiction, and a group of occasional pindarics on state or public events like the birth of the Pretender. Either the theater did not pay sufficiently well in these lean days, or she was ill or out of favor: the turn to fiction in the last two years of her life is indicative of her continued need for ready cash.

Her last year was marked by constant illness[23] and frantic attempts to provide herself with the necessities of life. *Oronooko* and a dozen other works show that she retained some of her great energy to the end. But such moving lines as those in the poem to Gilbert Burnet[24] indicate that she knew she had not long to live. Characteristically—and accurately—she joins her imminent death with the passing of the Stuart era.[25] Alone, crippled, impoverished, she died April 16, 1689. The writer of the "Memoirs" attributes death to "an unskilful physician" ([b7ᵛ]); Gildon describes her burial "in the cloisters of Westminster Abbey, under a plain marble stone, with two wretched verses for her epitaph, who had herself wrote so many good."[26]

Despite what has been written about her in the nearly three hundred years since her death, the character given her by the author of the "Memoirs" remains one of the best:

> She was of a generous and open temper, something passionate, very serviceable to her friends in all that was in her power, and could sooner forgive an injury than do one. She had wit, honor, good humor, and judgment. She was mistress of all the pleasing arts of conversation, but used 'em not to any but those who loved not [*sic*] plain dealing. She was a woman of sense, and by consequence a lover of pleasure, as indeed all . . . are; but only some would be thought to be above the conditions of humanity, and place their chief pleasure in a proud, vain hypocrisy. For my part, I knew her intimately, and never saw aught unbecoming the just modesty of our sex, tho' more gay and free than the folly of the precise will allow. She was, I'm satisfied, a greater honor to our sex than all the canting tribe of dissemblers that die with the false reputation of saints.
>
> ([b8]-[b8ᵛ])

Nothing in her works, or in what is known about her, suggests that this description is anything less than accurate.

CHAPTER 2

The Dramatist: Early Plays

I The Forced Marriage

MRS. Behn's first play, *The Forced Marriage; or, The Jealous Bridegroom*, was produced at Lincoln's Inn Fields in September, 1670, and printed in 1671.[1] Like many other plays in the early Restoration period, it belongs to the tradition of romantic tragicomedy established in the Jacobean period by the plays of Francis Beaumont and John Fletcher.

In the not especially complicated plot, the king of an Arcadian France, at the instigation of his son Philander, rewards the valor of Alcippus by making him general of the army. Alcippus makes a poor return by then asking for Erminia, to whom Philander is secretly betrothed. Her father Orgulius, recalled to favor through Philander's love, grants her to Alcippus, to the dismay of both Philander and the Princess Galatea, who secretly loves the new general.

After the wedding, Erminia remains faithful to Philander, and Alcippus grows more and more jealous. Their quarrel results in a fight, and eventually in Alcippus' strangling Erminia in a fit of rage and leaving her for dead. After a number of ghostly appearances by Erminia, ending in an elaborate masque, Alcippus resigns Erminia to Philander for Galatea and half a kingdom; and the play ends happily. The sub-plot involves the Beatrice and Benedick wooing of Alcander and Aminta, which is also resolved by marriage. A minor action unites the cowardly fop Falatius with the lady he has jilted.

The apparent theme of the play is the conflict between love and honor, a popular subject to which Mrs. Behn contributes little. Alcippus apparently loves Erminia to begin with, though his "love" is really mere infatuation. His honor suggests that the glory of marrying the princess offsets the loss of Erminia;

on the other hand, his honor suffers if Erminia is unfaithful, or denies him his marital rights. Erminia is similarly torn between the obedience and respect due her lawful husband, and her love for Philander. The prince must respect the law of which his father is the symbol, but Alcippus has wounded his honor and denied him his love.

Embodied in significant poetry such themes might have been made meaningful, but Mrs. Behn's treatment is superficial and not very poetic. For example, once Alcippus' honor is satisfied, he has no difficulty shifting his affections to Galatea; the business is clumsily handled and quite unconvincing. Erminia's conflict is also superficial: she is never really faced with the actual choice between love and honor, and in the play her love for Philander is in doubt only symbolically, when she agrees to pretend greater affection for Alcippus.

The theme which gives the play its title is more interesting. Mrs. Behn shows herself quite early to be an outspoken critic of arranged marriages forced on women without regard to love. Orgulius is deaf to Erminia's plea that she loves Philander, and she bows to her duty. Her soliloquy, however, reveals her real feelings:

> Ungrateful duty, whose uncivil pride
> By reason is not to be satisfied;
> Who even love's almighty power o'erthrows,
> Or dost on it too rigorous laws impose;
> Who bindest up our virtue too too straight,
> And on our honor lays too great a weight;
> Coward, whom nothing but thy power makes strong;
> Whom age and malice bred t'affright the young . . .

Galatea even argues in the debate over Alcippus' punishment (IV.vii) that Orgulius, in refusing Erminia's plea in order to serve the king, is responsible for her supposed murder. The king himself says it was not wisely done, and in a later speech makes himself the spokesman for Mrs. Behn's own view:

> Alas, Philander, I am old and feeble,
> And cannot long survive;
> But thou hast many ages yet to number

> Of youth and vigor, and should all be wasted
> In the embraces of an unloved maid?
> No, my Philander . . . (V.iii)

The idea that the socio-economic factors in marriage are designed to counteract the power of love in the interests of a stable society is interesting, and the thematic use of the concept in succeeding plays shows that Mrs. Behn was aware of its implications. Her appraisal of the established position is as accurate as Samuel Richardson's in *Clarissa,* and her attack on it at least as steady. One can, for example, judge the older characters in most of her plays by the side of the question they adopt. Mrs. Behn herself is always for the young and passionate; if she sometimes has her lovers marry, her interest, like Jane Austen's, ends with the proposal.

Strongly individualized characters are not a feature of *The Forced Marriage.* Pisaro is merely the faithful follower of Alcippus; Alcander, that of Philander. Alcippus is a passionate man, faintly reminiscent of the protagonists of the heroic plays so popular in the 1660's, but at its best his language is nearly empty rhetoric:

> Am I not tied a slave to follow love,
> Whilst at my back freedom and honor waits,
> And I have lost the power to welcome them?
> Like those who meet a devil in the night,
> And all affrighted gaze upon the fury,
> But dare not turn their backs to what they fear,
> Though safety lie behind them.
> Alas, I would as willingly as those
> Fly from this devil love. (IV.ii)

The elaboration of the simile is inappropriate to the mood of jealousy and passion which is supposed to motivate Alcippus in the scene.

The best characters, in fact, are the minor ones who figure in the comic action. Falatius is the type of the cowardly and foppish courtier, yet he is amusing; the dialogue between Aminta and Alcander pales beside that of Millamant and Mirabell, but is nevertheless successful:

> Here, take me, *Alcander,*
> Whilst to inconstancy I bid adieu;
> I find variety enough in you. (V.v)

The play is quite well constructed, especially for a first effort. There is always sufficient action on the stage; entrances and exits are managed with some economy; there is sufficient contrast between the scenes, and between the main and sub-plots, to maintain variety while advancing the central action. Even in construction, however, there are a number of weaknesses. For example, the story of Orgulius belongs to the exposition; yet it is brought in by a long speech of Galatea to Erminia in the middle of Act III. And the reader who could bear with such clumsy handling of structure could never tolerate having Mrs. Behn rouse his interest in a potentially serious theme, only to have her destroy it by an elaborate masque whose primary interest is obviously spectacle.

Nothing can make up for the stilted language of much of the play. Some scenes, usually those involving comedy or swordplay, are in prose; most are in an irregular blank verse; and more than a few are in sing-song couplets. The blank verse sometimes loses the feeling of pentameter entirely:

> Nor knew he other rest than on his horse-back;
> When he would sit and take a hearty nap,
> And then too dreamt of fighting.
> I could continue on a day in telling
> The wonders of this warrior. (I.i)

But the couplets are worse. They are nearly all end-stopped, and have no rhythmic variety at all:

> When your great soul a sorrow can admit,
> I ought to suffer from the sense of it;
> Your cause of grief too much like mine appears,
> Not to oblige my eyes to double tears;
> And had my heart no sentiments at home,
> My part in yours had doubtless filled the room. (I.ii)

Mrs. Behn was soon to learn that poetic drama was not her forte; in this play, only the songs merit the reader's attention as verse.

[32]

Despite its many weaknesses, *The Forced Marriage* ran for six nights, no mean number for the period.[2] The prologue makes modest claims for women—"Today one of their party ventures out, / Not with design to conquer, but to scout"—and the epilogue admits "we have promised what we could not do."[3] The modern reader is likely to take this literally and to regard the comparative success of the play as due to the excellence of the cast (the great actor Thomas Betterton and his wife played Alcippus and Erminia) and the audience's interest in the visual effects of the marriage and the masque.[4]

II   The Amorous Prince

The stage success of *The Forced Marriage* obviously encouraged its young author. She had to earn her living; and the stage, however capricious its audience, offered more certain rewards than espionage for the crown. Her second effort, produced at the Duke's Theatre in Lincoln's Inn Fields in February, 1671, was *The Amorous Prince; or, The Curious Husband.*[5] The prologue announces that the play is neither "regular" comedy of the Jonsonian sort nor farce, but "Th' imperfect issue of a lukewarm brain"—a description which is not so much inaccurate as unhelpful. The play has the double plot common in English tragicomedy, though the two strands are not very closely integrated.

The main plot is serious and romantic; like that of *The Forced Marriage,* it owes quite a bit to the Beaumont and Fletcher tradition. Cloris, for example, celebrates the beauty of the pastoral or rural life; and the contrast between her values and those of her urbane and often amoral seducer, the amorous Prince Frederick, is effectively managed. The seduction is accomplished with a promise of marriage, but Frederick soon becomes infatuated with Laura, who is betrothed to his close friend Curtius, Cloris' brother. Frederick and Curtius quarrel, giving Mrs. Behn the opportunity to develop the theme of love versus friendship which also figures in her first play. Curtius constructs an elaborate and highly theatrical plot to have Frederick killed in revenge for the dishonor to Cloris and the theft of Laura, but this plot is foiled; and the play ends happily with a penitent Frederick resigning Laura to Curtius and accepting Cloris in marriage.

The second plot is a version of the popular tale of the jealous husband's persuading his friend to test the fidelity of his wife.[6] Antonio is the husband; Clarina, the wife; Alberto, the friend. Mrs. Behn complicates the story by giving Clarina a sister, Ismena, who has exchanged identities with Clarina in order to win Alberto. The interest thus centers on the conflict between Alberto's love for "Clarina" and his friendship for Antonio; this thematic parallel and the comic character Lorenzo (Laura's brother, foolishly in love with Clarina) are the primary links between the two plots. Eventually Antonio, cured of his jealousy, is forgiven by his wife, and Ismena reveals her masquerade in time to be united with Alberto.

The Amorous Prince is obviously more complicated in plot than *The Forced Marriage*. While the tone of both plays is that of romantic comedy, one can see Mrs. Behn's movement toward greater reliance on plot devices and less on conventional themes, and toward the creation of theatrically effective spectacle rather than the stylized analysis of abstract ideas. The play is written in the same mixture of rough blank verse, prose, and couplets used in *The Forced Marriage*. The language here, however, is occasionally quite effective. Cloris, for example, brought up in rural seclusion, addresses Frederick in simple words appropriate to her character: "I know not what it is to dwell in courts, / But sure it must be fine, since you are there . . ." (I.i). Such moments are rare, however; Mrs. Behn's talent is for comedy rather than romance, and the best language in the play occurs in the plausible and rapid dialogue, particularly that involving the extravagant fop Lorenzo:

GUILLIOM.
As for fighting, though I do not care for it, yet I can do't if anybody angers me or so.

LORENZO.
But I must have you learn to do't when anybody angers me, too.

GUILLIOM.
Sir, they told me I should have no need on't here; but I shall learn.

LORENZO.
Why you fool, that's not a thing to be learned!
That's a brave inclination born with man;

A brave undaunted something, a thing that,
That—comes from—from—I know not what,
For I was born without it.   (III.iii)

The play is generally well constructed, and in some ways marks a distinct advance over *The Forced Marriage*. For example, in the earlier play the elaborate masque occurs in Act V, scene ii, and has a fairly tenuous and certainly not inevitable structural function: it provides Alcippus with an opportunity to display his emotional turmoil, and encourages him to marry Galatea. In *The Amorous Prince* the masque occurs at the beginning of the last scene, and, as Henry Hargreaves notes (pp. 108-09), is much more closely integrated with the unraveling of complications the play has set up. Mrs. Behn also keeps most of the exposition in the first two acts, and makes the denouement more convincing by having it depend on something more than a sudden change in affection. The prince, one feels, has loved Cloris all along; he merely faces up to it in the end. And, since Alberto has been wooing Ismena from the start, all that is required for a convincing ending is her revelation of her true identity. The actors' names are unknown, but the rapid and often entertaining plot, workmanlike dialogue, and careful construction must have helped ensure a moderate run.

III   The Dutch Lover

Mrs. Behn's third play, *The Dutch Lover*, was first performed in February, 1673, at the Duke's new theater in Dorset Garden.[7] The cast of actors is unknown, but it is clear from the author's preface to the printed version (1673) that the play was not a success. Her reply to her critics begins with a gibe at the incomprehensibility of seventeenth-century Puritan cant, and with a modest defense of the value of plays:

I would not yet be understood to lessen the dignity of plays, for surely they deserve a place among the middle, if not the better sort of books. For I have heard that most of that which bears the name of learning, and which has abused such quantities of ink and paper, and continually employs so many ignorant, unhappy souls for ten, twelve, twenty years in the university (who yet, poor wretches, think they are doing something all the while)—as logic, etc., and several other things (that shall be nameless, lest I should misspell them)—are much more absolutely nothing than the errantest play that e'er was writ. ([A2^v])

She then asserts that plays do not really reform men or manners, thus surrendering the mainstay of those apologists concerned with defending Puritan attacks on the immorality of the stage. Her simple argument is entirely convincing: those who frequent the playhouse "make the fondest and the lewdest crew about this town; for if you should unhappily converse them through the year, you will not find one dram of sense amongst a club of them . . ." ([A3]).[8] Indeed, she very cleverly puts plays and sermons in the same category:

. . . In my judgment the increasing number of our latter plays have not done much more towards the amending of men's morals, or their wit, than hath the frequent preaching, which this last age hath been pestered with, . . . nor can I once imagine what temptation anyone can have to expect it from them: for, sure I am, no play was ever writ with that design. If you consider tragedy, you'll find their best of characters unlikely patterns for a wise man to pursue. . . . And as for comedy, the finest folks you meet with there, are still unfitter for your imitation. . . . Nor is this error very lamentable, since as I take it comedy was never meant, either for a converting or a confirming ordinance. In short, I think a play the best divertisement that wise men have; but I do also think them nothing so, who do discourse as formally about the rules of it, as if 'twere the grand affair of human life. This being my opinion of plays, I studied only to make this as entertaining as I could, which, whether I have been successful in, my gentle reader, you may for your shilling judge.
([A3^v]-[A4])

Mrs. Behn, as her words suggest, was not interested in dramatic theory, or in deducing her stagecraft from rules of any sort. She wrote to amuse the audiences of her day; if the play succeeded, she was satisfied; if it failed, she accepted the judgment of the pit—if her work had had a fair trial. *The Dutch Lover*, she protests, did not. She implies in the Epistle that the critics objected to her work because she was a woman who, among other things, had no learning:

Indeed, that day 'twas acted first, there comes me into the pit, a long, lither, phlegmatic, white, ill-favored, wretched fop, an officer in masquerade newly transported . . . out of France, a sorry animal that has nought else to shield it from the uttermost contempt of all mankind, but that respect which we afford to rats and toads, which though we do not well allow to live, yet when considered as a part of God's creation, we make honorable mention of them. A thing, reader—but no more of such a smelt. This thing, I tell ye, opening that which serves it for a mouth, out issued such a noise as this to those that sat about it, that they were to expect a woeful play, God damn him, for it was a woman's.   ([A4ᵛ])

Shakespeare, she says, pleases more than Jonson, yet has less learning. She feels she can write as well as any living man except Dryden: good plays do not require scholarship or rules no matter what Shadwell and his school say:

Then for their musty rules of unity, and God knows what besides, if they meant anything, they are enough intelligible, and as practible by a woman; but really methinks they that disturb their heads with any other rule of plays besides the making them pleasant, and avoiding of scurrility, might much better be employed in studying how to improve men's too too imperfect knowledge of that ancient English game which hight long Laurence. And if comedy should be the picture of ridiculous mankind, I wonder any one should think it such a sturdy task, whilst we are furnished with such precious originals as him I lately told you of, if at least that character do not dwindle into farce, and so become too mean an entertainment for those persons who are used to think.   (al-[alᵛ])

Having answered this *ad hominem* attack on her play, she complains that it "was hugely injured in the acting" ([alᵛ]). The actors were imperfect in their parts, the Dutch Lover ad-libbed "idle stuff" and lacked a sufficiently ridiculous and distinguishing costume, and the person who promised her the epilogue deputed the task to an inferior writer.

There is no reason to doubt that Mrs. Behn's complaints were justified, for *The Dutch Lover* is a much better play than its two predecessors. There are still marks of the apprentice, but the conception is larger and the execution better than in anything she had so far done. The play is clearly transitional; it marks the end of her reliance on the Beaumont and Fletcher tradition; and its emphasis on adventure and intrigue, interspersed with both witty dialogue and farce, is typical of the pattern its author was to follow with very few exceptions until the end of her career.

The plot is based on *The History of Don Fenise*, a contemporary novel. As she says in the Epistle, it is "busy"; four different sets of lovers are involved in the serious plot, and three more in the comic. One line of action concerns Roderigo, son of the disgraced Count d'Olivarez, who has been brought up by the count's friend Don Ambrosio as his own natural son Silvio, and given a place beside his other children Cleonte, Hippolita, and Marcel. Silvio's supposedly incestuous love for Cleonte is resolved after many turns by Don Ambrosio's revelation of his true identity. The situation has many parallels in previous drama: Ford's *'Tis Pity She's a Whore* uses it for tragedy, Beaumont and Fletcher's *A King and No King*, for tragicomedy.

Another plot concerns Alonzo's love for Don Carlo's daughter Euphemia, who picks him as a substitute for the comic Haunce. Alonzo is eventually found to be Don Manuel's missing heir; his inheritance wins Don Carlo's consent to his marriage, and Don Ambrosio's consent to Marcel's marriage with his newly revealed sister Clarinda. Finally, Antonio admits his love for Hippolita, whom he has seduced, and Ambrosio gives them his blessing. Haunce and his tutor Gload are tricked into marrying Euphemia's maids, and Pedro takes up again with his long-lost mistress Dormida.

The dovetailing of so many plot strands is, on the whole, very carefully done. The revelations come in Act V, and the explanation of identities must be followed closely for several scenes. But, given good staging and costuming, there would be small chance of real confusion. It is not clear where Antonio comes from in Act II.ii, or how Francisca knows Marcel has arrived in II.vi; but these are minor flaws.

As the summary suggests, the Silvio-Cleonte and Hippolita-Antonio plots are still romantic tragicomedy. Hippolita's soliloquy as she watches Antonio sleep is one of many passages in this vein. However, the diction is clearer, the figurative language more apt, and the feeling of the character more convincingly portrayed than in the earlier plays:

[38]

HIPPOLITA.

Why should this villain sleep, this treacherous man,
Who has for ever robbed me of my rest?
Had I but kept my innocence entire,
I had out-braved my fate, and broke my chains,
Which now bear like a poor guilty slave,
Who sadly cries, "If I were free from these,
I am not from my crimes"; so still lives on,
And drags his loathed fetters after him.
Why should I fear to die, or murder him?
It is but adding one sin more to th' number.
This would soon do't—   *Draws a dagger, sighs.*
                         But where's the hand to guide it?
For 'tis an act too horrid for a woman.   *Turns away.*
But yet thus sleeping I might take that soul, *Turns to him.*
Which, waking, all the charms of art and nature
Had not power t'effect.   (III.iii)

But duels indoors and out, mistaken identities, disguises, mixed-up assignations, and of course Haunce van Ezel, give a very different tone to the play as a whole. The number of plots and their intricate fusing are clear signs of the influence of Spanish intrigue comedy introduced into England by Sir Samuel Tuke's *Adventures of Five Hours* (1663), which Samuel Pepys called "a play of the greatest plot that ever I expect to see."[9] Variety of incident is more important in *The Dutch Lover* than Silvio's passion; Alonzo's adventures stay with the reader longer than Marcel's jealousy and anger. Mrs. Behn obviously likes intrigue comedy: if she began working with it because it was popular, she continued after the fashion faded. Its complexity permitted full display of her superior craftsmanship; its emphasis on incident allowed her to develop comedy primarily through action and situation rather than through character and language; its many plots offered a chance to appeal to romance, intrigue, manners, and farce in the same play, and to indulge her interest in spectacle.

The farcical scenes involving Haunce van Ezel, although they give the play its title, are of secondary importance. Alonzo disguises himself as Haunce to woo Euphemia, but the real Haunce does not appear until the middle of the play (III.ii). He figures importantly in five scenes, ending the play on a comic note. His presence may be related to the renewal of the

Dutch war in 1672, and may owe something to Mrs. Behn's experience as a spy in Holland. George Woodcock, indeed, says that he "is clearly derived from fairly accurate observation of a certain type of seventeenth-century Dutchman,"[10] and the amount of detail in Gload's description of him (III.ii) lends some credence to the observation. In the play, however, Haunce is treated as a stock comic fool.

At least as interesting as Haunce are elements of the comedy of wit, centering in the character of Alonzo. Despite his Spanish name, he is the first of Mrs. Behn's gay blades: fond of women but not of constancy, game for any intrigue. A sure sign of his presence is the comic reversal of values connected with that key institution of society—marriage. When he tells Lovis he is in Madrid to marry Hippolita, Lovis makes a characteristic reply: "Nay, then keep her to thyself, only let me know who 'tis can debauch thee to that scandalous way of life . . . ?" And Alonzo admits he's not as brisk as he might be: "I have been used to Christian liberty, and hate this formal courtship" (I.i.). However, one look at Euphemia wins the day, and he is willing to pay her price.

One may note in conclusion that *The Dutch Lover* continues Mrs. Behn's interest in stage and sound effects. There is a brief masquerade in Act V.ii that is used to dispose of Haunce and Gload to the two maids, and a pastoral masque is used by Silvio in III.vi to lure Cleonte into his arms. There is music at several points in the play, and a dance by Haunce's ship's company in IV.i. *The Dutch Lover* also contains two of its author's best poems, fitted with great care into the situations in which they appear (II.vi and III.iii). The delicacy and skill of Hippolita's song to the sleeping Antonio is a fine example of the Restoration lyric:

> Ah, false Amyntas, can that hour
> So soon forgotten be,
> When first I yielded up my power
> To be betrayed by thee?
> God knows with how much innocence
> I did my heart resign,
> Unto thy faithless eloquence,
> And gave thee what was mine. (III.iii)

CHAPTER 3

The Dramatist: Mid-Career

THE failure of *The Dutch Lover* may have temporarily discouraged Mrs. Behn from writing for the stage. At least, she is not known to have produced any plays between February, 1673, and about July, 1676, when *Abdelazer* was produced at the Duke's Theatre in Dorset Garden.[1] In fact, no known works in any genre date from this period, and her activities are a matter for speculation. The period between July, 1676, and March, 1682, on the other hand, is certainly the most important in her career and probably the most productive. No less than eleven plays known to be hers, and three which she may have done, were produced in the five and one-half years; and all but one were printed. They include five of the seven or eight plays for which she deserves to be remembered, and most of those by which the Restoration and early eighteenth century knew her.

I Abdelazer

The popularity of romantic tragedy in the Restoration is certainly shown by *Abdelazer*, for only the hope of substantial income is likely to have persuaded her to attempt something so remote from her real abilities. The plot closely follows the anonymous sixteenth century play *Lust's Dominion*, from which it was adapted. Abdelazer, son of a Moorish king killed by the king of Spain, has been adopted and made a general. His ruling passion is revenge, however; and, to further it, he becomes the lover of the lascivious Queen Isabella and helps her kill the king. Her younger son Philip publicly accuses her of adultery, and Abdelazer is banished by Cardinal Mendozo, protector of the new king Ferdinand. Ferdinand, however, loves Abdelazer's wife Florella; and he revokes the cardinal's edict. Philip and Mendozo escape the Moor's vengeance, and Ferdinand's attempts to seduce Florella eventually result in her death at the hands of the jealous Isabella and his at the hands of Abdelazer.

When Philip becomes king, Abdelazer and the queen announce falsely that he is a bastard; and the former is accepted unwillingly as Protector. Alonzo, Florella's brother, carries the news to Philip, and a battle between his army and Abdelazer's is won by the Moor thanks to the defection of Mendozo, who loves Isabella. At court, the Queen asserts Mendozo to be Philip's father, but he denies the lie and is arrested for treason. The Infanta Leonora is proclaimed queen, and Abdelazer has Isabella killed so he can be free to woo her. He wounds Osmin, his faithful officer, when the latter interrupts his rape of Leonora with news that her betrothed Alonzo has been captured. In revenge, Osmin frees Philip, Mendozo, and Alonzo. When Abdelazer comes to kill them, they attack him and he dies after killing Osmin, still boasting of his misdeeds. Mendozo is forgiven, Philip becomes king, and Alonzo marries Leonora.

The play has fine moments. The opening scene, in which Abdelazer muses beside a table—here the superb lyric "Love in Fantastic Triumph Sat" is sung—and then reproaches Isabella for having wasted his youth and made him a mere gigolo, is an example. Also, Abdelazer's single-minded devotion to revenge is fairly well motivated, since the Spanish had killed his father. He echoes the villains of the heroic drama more than once in his capacity for pure evil:

> Now all that's brave and villain seize my soul,
> Reform each faculty that is not ill,
> And make it fit for vengeance, noble vengeance!
> Oh glorious word, fit only for the gods,
> For which they formed their thunder;
> Till man usurped their power, and by revenge
> Swayed destiny as well as they,
> And took their trade of killing.
> And thou, almighty love,
> Dance in a thousand forms about my person,
> That this same Queen, this easy Spanish dame,
> May be bewitched, and dote upon me still;

Whilst I make use of the insatiate flame
To set all Spain on fire.
Mischief, erect thy throne,
And sit on high; here, here upon my head.   (I.i)

Although Abdelazer's character must carry the play, he comes alive only by fits and starts. The scene in the presence chamber during which he proclaims Leonora queen (V.i.) is superbly handled: he outwits the cardinal and imposes his will on the court without ever deviating from the ceremonious language appropriate to the occasion. Yet he is often a mere personification of revenge, and especially so in the final scene. After gloating over his successes in a rather mechanical fashion, he indulges himself in a final—and extremely artificial—epic simile which lasts all of ten lines.

Queen Isabella is a study in the corrupting power of lust. To it, she sacrifices her husband, her children, and her country; from it, she gains a few weeks in Abdelazer's arms before her wretched death. But Mrs. Behn cannot bring her off. In much of the play, she feigns a part; and her conventional rhetoric conceals her real attitude very well. Her passion for Abdelazer, however, has the same rhetorical character; the reader rarely believes in it because he cannot really believe in her. In Act II, scene i she tells us that love is stronger than nature in her soul, and she justifies her hedonism in the face of what she calls the hypocrisy of the virtuous. Mrs. Behn keeps her quite consistent, carefully showing that her love is entirely selfish lust, although it is often subservient to the desire for revenge on anyone who thwarts her. Yet she remains thinly conceived: exhibiting few symptoms of guilt or suffering even in her quarrels with Abdelazer. We see her much as we see Lyndaraxa in *The Conquest of Granada,* but she lacks the intensity and vivid language with which Dryden invests his creation.

The staging calls for elaborate costumes and ingenious changes of scene, and the play is full of spectacle—a coronation, a full-scale battle, and a dozen murders to titillate the audience. Henry Purcell, the greatest English composer of the century, provided the music,[2] and Thomas Betterton, the greatest actor of the age, played the title role. Mrs. Betterton, Mrs.

Barry and Mrs. Lee acted Florella, Leonora, and Isabella, respectively. With such advantages, the play was successful in its first run, and was even chosen as the first play at the reopening of Drury Lane in the spring of 1695.

But there is no reason, as there is in the case of *The Town Fop*, to question its subsequent neglect; the turgid rhetoric destroys scene after scene. Mrs. Behn lacks Thomas Otway's ability to sustain an elevated diction through a whole scene, and she is incapable of the magnificent prosody and the organizing images which quicken the best of Dryden's heroic plays. Abdelazer and Isabella are potentially complex and interesting, but the author cannot invest them with the language requisite for tragedy. *Abdelazer* must have been a fascinating experiment, but she was wise never to repeat it.

II The Town Fop

In *The Town Fop*, produced about September, 1676, at Dorset Garden,[3] romantic tragicomedy has disappeared. The play is partly a comedy of intrigue and partly one of manners. Mrs. Behn's first play set in London, it is full of realistic scenes of city life.

The plot, based on George Wilkins' play *The Miseries of Enforced Marriage*, is rather less complicated than that of *The Dutch Lover*, but it again involves several strands of action and a number of disguises. Lord Plotwell has four wards—Bellmour, Diana, Charles, and Phillis—and now insists that Bellmour marry Diana. Bellmour, however, is secretly betrothed to Celinda, Celinda's brother Friendlove is in love with Diana, and her parents intend Celinda for the fop Sir Timothy Tawdrey. To save his inheritance, Bellmour agrees to marry Diana; and the ceremony is performed. He writes Celinda, who pretends she has taken poison and then disguises herself as a boy to protect Bellmour from Friendlove, who believes he has been betrayed.

On the wedding night, Bellmour repulses Diana's advances and she vows revenge. She looks for a man to kill her husband in return for her favors, and finally secures the disguised Friendlove. In dissipation in a brothel, Bellmour gives full vent to his anguish over Celinda's "death." When his brother Charles eventually finds him, the two quarrel and Charles is wounded. When Lord Plotwell hears of Bellmour's conduct, he resolves to help

Diana secure a divorce. Meanwhile, Sir Timothy, repulsed early in the play by Celinda and not satisfied with his mistress Betty Flauntit, pursues Phillis. Through the agency of Trusty, Lord Plotwell's faithful steward, he is tricked into marrying her. The event paves the way for Bellmour: Lord Plotwell forgives him; Diana divorces him to marry her champion, now revealed as Friendlove; and Celinda—also unmasked—will be his as soon as the divorce is received.

The play is constructed carefully and well, but to her usual craftsmanship Mrs. Behn adds more probable and interesting characters and excellent dialogue. The opening scene between Sir Timothy and his hangers-on Sharp and Sham is one of many examples revealing the author's now considerable skill in defining characters and their environment through rhythm, diction, and imagery:

Sir Timothy.

Your pardon, sweet Sharp; my whole design in it is to be master of myself, and with part of her portion to set up my miss, Betty Flaunt-it; which, by the way is the main end of my marrying. The rest you'll have your shares of. Now I am forced to take you up suits at treble prices, have damned wine and meat put upon us, 'cause the reckoning is to be booked. But ready money, ye rogues, what charms it has! Makes the waiters fly, boys, and the master with cap in hand: "Excuse what's amiss, gentlemen, your worship shall command the best." And the rest—how briskly the box and dice dance, and the ready money submits to the lucky gamester, and the gay wench consults with every beauty to make herself agreeable to the man with ready money! In fine, dear rogues, all things are sacrificed to power, and no mortal conceives the joy of *argent content*. 'Tis this powerful God that makes me submit to the devil matrimony; and then thou art assured of me, my stout lads of brisk debauch.

Sham.

And is it possible you can be tied up to a wife? Whilst here in London, and free, you have the whole world to range in, and, like a wanton heifer, eat of every pasture?

Sir Timothy.

Why, dost think I'll be confined to my own dull enclosure? No, I had rather feed coarsely upon the boundless common. Perhaps two or three days I may be in love, and remain constant, but that's the most.

SHARP.
And in three weeks, should you wed a Cinthia, you'd be a monster.

SIR TIMOTHY.
What, thou meanest a cuckold, I warrant? God help thee! But a monster is only so from its rarity, and a cuckold is no such strange thing in our age. (I.i)

The whole play is as rapidly paced as this scene; interest never flags; and speeches of more than four or five lines, unless purely comic, are the exception.

Sir Timothy himself is the complete fop: exposed to the ridicule of everyone from Celinda's old nurse (I.ii) to his own mistress Betty Flauntit (V.i), he is at once a convincing dramatic character and a useful vehicle for the comic examination of contemporary manners:

SIR TIMOTHY.
Fair maid—

PHILLIS.
How do you know that, Sir?

SIR TIMOTHY.
I see y'are fair, and I guess you're a maid.

PHILLIS.
Your guess is better than your eyesight, Sir.

SIR TIMOTHY.
Whate'er you are, by Fortune, I wish you would permit me to love you with all faults.

PHILLIS.
You? Pray, who are you?

SIR TIMOTHY.
A man, a gentleman—and more, a knight, too, by Fortune.

PHILLIS.
Then 'twas not by merit, Sir. But how shall I know you are either of these?

SIR TIMOTHY.
That I'm a man, the effects of my vigorous flame shall prove; a gentleman, my coat of arms shall testify; and I have the King's patent for my title.

PHILLIS.

For the first you may thank your youth, for the next your father, and the last your money.

SIR TIMOTHY.

By Fortune, I love thee for thy pertness.

PHILLIS.

Is it possible you can love at all?

SIR TIMOTHY.

As much as I dare.

PHILLIS.

How d'ye mean?

SIR TIMOTHY.

Not to be laughed at. T'is not the mode to love much: A platonic fop I have heard of, but this is an age of sheer enjoyment, and little love goes to that; we have found it incommode, and loss of time, to make long addresses. (III.i)

Betty Flauntit and her companions are just as accurately drawn and equally funny: the scene in the brothel (IV.ii) is a minor masterpiece; it examines custom and fashion on one social level by mirroring it on another:

FLAUNTIT.

Lord, they think there are such joys in keeping, when I vow, Driver, after a while, a miss has as painful a life as a wife: our men drink, stay out late, and whore, like any husbands.

DRIVER.

But I hope in the Lord, Mrs. Flauntit, yours is no such man. I never saw him, but I have heard he is under decent correction.

Opposed to the amorality of the fops, whores, and sharpers are the true lovers, who must pick their way through a society full of false values and fashionable phrases. Sir Timothy is the foil against which the audience measures the genuine devotion of Bellmour to Celinda and of Friendlove to Diana, just as Trusty shows up Sham and Sharp. Since this is the world of comedy, Bellmour and Friendlove arrive happily at their goals. But the comedy is strongly realistic: Sir Timothy, married to Phillis, will use her portion to set up Betty in style; and, if Sham and

[47]

Sharp have served Trusty's purposes, they have done so for a price.

The Town Fop continues Mrs. Behn's interest in effective theater. In Act III.i "Music plays, till they are all seated," and there is a wedding dance, which Sir Timothy, Friendlove, and others attend in masquerade. In III.iii Sir Timothy has the newly married couple serenaded, and in IV.i Diana sings to the disguised Celinda. Scene changes are frequent, entrances and exits are carefully worked out, and there is the usual complement of sword play and mistaken identities.

Concern for the theatrical does not, however, draw attention away from the more meaningful aspects of the play, as it did in *The Forced Marriage* and occasionally does in later plays. In fact, *The Town Fop* is more closely integrated in structure than any previous play. Mrs. Behn creates Friendlove in order to have a pair of friends to match the pair of heroines; she obviously likes the complications that can be produced by entangling the two sets of relationships, but she also likes the structural balance it furnishes. Her efforts were probably appreciated: The play was licensed on September 20, 1676; and *The London Stage* records a performance as late as November.[4]

III The Rover

The Rover; or, The Banished Cavaliers, adapted from Thomas Killigrew's *Thomaso* and first produced at the Duke's Theatre in Dorset Garden in March, 1677,[5] is Mrs. Behn's most famous play, and one of her best. Set in Naples during Carnival, it presents the adventures of a group of cavaliers: Willmore (the Rover), Belvile, Frederick, and Ned Blunt. Belvile, who saved Florinda and her brother Pedro at the siege of Pamplona, has fallen in love with her. Her sister Hellena, destined for the convent, finds out her secret; and the two go to the Carnival with their old nurse Callis and their cousin Valeria, all in masquerade. Florinda, who is intended by her father for old Vincentio and by Pedro for his friend Antonio, arranges to meet Belvile instead. Hellena falls in love with Willmore, and Valeria with Frederick. The cavaliers next encounter the famous courtesan Angelica Bianca; and, while Antonio and Pedro dispute over her, the penniless Willmore wins her with his charm and enjoys her favors gratis. But, when he continues to woo Hellena, he arouses Angelica's jealousy and wrath. After some very complicated machinations involving fights, disguises, mistaken identities, and so on, Angelica departs in fury, Antonio resigns his claims to Belvile and Pedro accepts their marriage. Frederick is united to Valeria, and Willmore to Hellena. Even Ned Blunt, picked clean by a prostitute he took for a lady, gets over his discomfiture at last.

The tone of the play is set by Willmore; his gaiety and rather amoral attitude toward life make him the very type of the Restoration gallant. He is for any adventure and any beautiful woman, so long as the adventure is not dishonorable and the woman not set on marriage. He can be won only by Hellena, whose freshness, wit, and beauty allay his fears of bondage— and he tries every persuasion he knows before capitulating. He sums himself up in a speech to Angelica:

> I wish I were that dull, that constant thing
> Which thou wouldst have, and nature never meant me;
> I must, like cheerful birds, sing in all groves
> And perch on every bough,
> Billing the next kind she that flies to meet me;
> Yet after all could build my nest with thee,
> Thither repairing when I'd loved my round,
> And still reserve a tributary flame.   (V.i)

And, when the die is cast, he faces marriage in his own characteristic way, accepting it as a challenge:

WILLMORE.
But hast thou no better quality to recommend thyself by?

HELLENA.
Faith, none, Captain. Why, 'twill be the greater charity to take me for thy mistress. I am a lone child, a kind of orphan lover, and why I should die a maid, and in a captain's hands too, I do not understand.

WILLMORE.
Egad, I was never clawed away with broadsides from any female before. Thou hast one virtue I adore, good nature; I hate a coy, demure mistress; she's as troublesome as a colt; I'll break none. No,

give me a mad mistress when mewed, and in flying on I dare trust upon the wing, that whilst she's kind will come to the lure.

HELLENA.

Nay, as kind as you will, good Captain, whilst it lasts, but let's lose no time.

WILLMORE.

My time's as precious to me as thine can be. Therefore, dear creature, since we are so well agreed, let's retire to my chamber, and if ever thou wert treated with such savory love! Come, my bed's prepared for such a guest all clean and sweet as thy fair self. I love to steal a dish and a bottle with a friend, and hate long graces. Come, let's retire and fall to.

HELLENA.

'Tis but getting my consent, and the business is soon done. Let but old gaffer Hymen and his priest say amen to it, and I dare lay my mother's daughter by as proper a fellow as your father's son, without fear or blushing.

WILLMORE.

Hold, hold, no bug words, child! Priest and Hymen? Prithee add a hangman to 'em to make up the consort. No, no, we'll have no vows but love, child, nor witness but the lover. The kind deity enjoins naught but love and enjoy! Hymen and priest wait still upon portion and jointure; love and beauty have their own ceremonies; marriage is as certain a bane to love, as lending money is to friendship. I'll neither ask nor give a vow, though I could be content to turn gipsy, and become a left-handed bridegroom, to have the pleasure of working that great miracle of making a maid a mother, if you durst venture. 'Tis upse gipsy that, and if I miss, I'll lose my labor.

HELLENA.

And if you do not lose, what shall I get? A cradle full of noise and mischief, with a pack of repentance at my back? Can you teach me to weave incle to pass my time with? 'Tis upse gipsy that, too.

WILLMORE.

I can teach thee to weave a true love's knot better.

HELLENA.

So can my dog.

WILLMORE.

Well, I see we are both upon our guards, and I see there's no way to conquer good nature, but by yielding. Here give me thy hand—one kiss and I am thine.

HELLENA.

One kiss! How like my page he speaks! I am resolved you shall have none, for asking such a sneaking sum. He that will be satisfied with one kiss, will never die of that longing. Good friend single-kiss, is all your talking come to this? A kiss, a caudle! Farewell, Captain Single-kiss. *Going out; he stays her.*

WILLMORE.

Nay, if we part so, let me die like a bird upon a bough, at the sheriff's charge. By heaven, both the Indies shall not buy thee from me. I adore thy humor and will marry thee, and we are so of one humor, it must be a bargain. Give me thy hand. *(Kisses her hand.)* And now let the blind ones (love and fortune) do their worst. (V.i)

In this passage several characteristics of Mrs. Behn's mature comedy appear: the handsome, carefree gallant, the frank and witty heroine, and a sparkling dialogue laced with comic images from everyday life. The sophistication and polish of Congreve are often missing; in their stead one finds a more earthy gaiety and vividness. As the quotation shows, *The Rover* is, in the Willmore-Hellena plot, a comedy of wit. Indeed, much of the action can be seen in these terms. Belvile is the faithful lover of a faithful Florinda; neither is especially witty, and the pair constitutes an effective foil to Willmore and Hellena, giving the play balance. Henry Hargreaves suggests (pp. 134-35) that Willmore, especially in his cups, is buffoon enough to resemble Sir Timothy in *The Town Fop*, and that Belvile is "the ideal lover." It seems to me, however, that the Rover is clearly the main character and that Mrs. Behn's sympathies are with him. Belvile is a stock "ideal" rather than a norm; or, at the least, Willmore is presented as an equally attractive norm. Frederick and Valeria are not significant, but do offer another comparison.

Opposed to the cavaliers is Ned Blunt, the country fool one sees in most of Mrs. Behn's comedies. Like Willmore, he follows his appetites; but, in place of Willmore's intelligence, vitality, and wit, he has only good nature. He is gulled because he is stupid and self-deceived: love for him is entirely carnal, to be bought and sold. The contrast between Willmore's motives in trying to gain Angelica and Blunt's in pursuing Lucetta illuminates the whole play; the low comedy plot is integral to the structure, not merely added in for relief.

[51]

It is also typical of Mrs. Behn that the comedy of wit element is presented within a comedy of intrigue framework. Ned Blunt's function has its parallel in manners plays, but the farcical manner in which he is duped does not. Pedro and Antonio are typical intrigue figures, and the masquerading, fighting, and confusion of identities are obvious intrigue devices. The more "romantic" or lurid aspects of intrigue comedy are seen in Angelica, who brandishes a pistol at Willmore for much of one scene and threatens murder with every other breath. With this character, indeed, the author is not entirely successful. Her passion is not really comic, for she has been too far revealed from the inside. She belongs to the world of *Abdelazer*, not to that of *The Rover*, and the two worlds jar when brought together.

On the stage, the play was Aphra Behn's most celebrated success and became part of the repertoire of the company. Smith, the original Willmore, and Underhill, the original Ned Blunt, were especially famous for their roles and recreated them many times. Thomas Betterton played Belvile; Mrs. Betterton, Florinda; Elizabeth Barry, Hellena; and Anne Quin, Angelica Bianca. The play remained popular longer than any other by its author: Will Mountford was another famous Rover; and Anne Bracegirdle, Ann Oldfield, and Peg Woffington were later Hellenas.[6] The last revival opened at Covent Garden in February, 1757, and the play was still successful enough for ten performances. By the end of the century, however, the public required less frank and open fare; John Phillip Kemble's altered version, presented at Drury Lane in 1790 under the title *Love in Many Masks*, has very little of the rollicking tone of the original. The epilogue to the original play hints of its eventual fate:

> The devil's in't if this will please the nation,
> In these our blessed times of reformation,
> When conventicling is so much in fashion.

IV Sir Patient Fancy

Sir Patient Fancy, produced at Dorset Garden in January, 1678,[7] is one of the best of the English adaptations of Molière. Though the author says in the address "To the Reader" in the printed version (1678) that she "had but a very bare hint from one, the *Malade imaginaire*," her play owes a great deal to *L'amour médicin* and *Les femmes savantes* as well as to *Le malade imaginaire* for characterization, incident, and detail. Such adaptation is the rule rather than the exception in the Restoration; plays like *Sir Patient Fancy* must be judged on their own merits rather than on the percentage of material created by their authors. Mrs. Behn's comedy dispenses with the economy, the controlling idea or character, and the special tone which identify Molière. As D. H. Miles has observed, "the minor dramatists were not studying the French genius as a master, but were delving into his works just as Scarron and Rotrou delved into the inexhaustible mine of Spanish comedy.... It is therefore only fair to judge them by their success in making the borrowed material suit their purposes."[8]

Mrs. Behn takes incidents, but not themes or methods. Her typically English play is based not on a single dominating conception but on the rich variety of incident and complication typical of intrigue comedy.[9] Sir Patient, father of Fanny and Isabella and uncle of Leander, has taken a young wife Lucia. She pretends to share the old alderman's pious cant and to humor his hypochondria, but secretly intrigues with her penniless gallant, Charles Wittmore. Surprised by her husband while talking with Wittmore, she introduces her lover as Fainlove, a suitor to Isabella; and the old man accepts him as such. Isabella, however, has promised herself to Lodwick, son of the comic bluestocking Lady Knowell. Lodwick's sister Lucretia loves Leander, but is being forced by her mother to marry the foolish country knight Sir Credulous Easy. After a complicated but highly amusing set of intrigues centering on Sir Patient's religiosity and hypochondria, Lady Knowell's pedantry, and Sir Credulous' gullibility, the lovers carry the day. Isabella marries Lodwick, Lady Knowell resigns Leander to Lucretia while Sir Credulous looks on, and Lucia casually plans to take the money her husband has settled on her to carry on her amour with Wittmore. Sir Patient, wiser but no sadder, plans to "turn Spark, . . . keep some City mistress, go to court, and hate all conventicles" (V.i).

Despite a few loose ends, the play is a fine one, combining within its intrigue framework a considerable amount of witty dialogue; analysis of contemporary manners; satire on such topics as Puritanism, mercenary marriages, and pedantry; and obvious but very funny farce. All of these elements are managed without confusion and with superior technical skill. The opening scene between Isabella and Lucretia, for example, not only introduces the two neighbor families, acquaints the reader with Isabella's love for Lodwick and Lucretia's for Leander, and places and briefly characterizes Sir Credulous, Lady Knowell, Lucia and Sir Patient; it also establishes the tone and milieu of the action through the girls' remarks about arranged marriages, foppery, pedantry, and the battle of the sexes—all in fewer than three pages. It is difficult to imagine more perfect exposition.

The characters are equally good. Lady Knowell lacks the exclusive comic trait of a Mrs. Malaprop, but she is almost as funny and rather more fully presented: her pedantry is one part of her, not the whole. While she can use Latin and Greek tags by the dozen, throughout amusing the audience with her "learning," she can also shrewdly pretend love to Leander to test his affection for Lucretia, and win her running battle with Sir Patient to the bargain. Sir Credulous, the perfect country bumpkin, is the dupe of one scheme after another, betraying his folly in every speech he makes:

SIR CREDULOUS.
For you must know, bright lady, though I was pleased to rally myself, I have a pretty competent estate of about £3000 a year, and am to marry Madam Lucretia.

LADY FANCY.
You're a happy man, Sir.

SIR CREDULOUS.
Not so happy neither, inestimable lady, for I lost the finest mare yesterday—but let that pass. . . .   (II.i)

But Sir Patient himself is the finest of the comic creations. His hypochondria may come from *Le malade imaginaire,* but he is pure English, the typical Whiggish merchant seen from the high Tory point of view. A pious Puritan who is only too happy to shift his devotions to liquor and sex when nightly prayers are called off, he is at once opinionated and stubborn where the marriages of his daughter and nephew are concerned, and foolishly deluded in his own. Yet he is never contemptible or pathetic. Mrs. Behn always makes her fools and fops human, and sometimes even shrewd. One feels that cuckolding has improved Sir Patient, and that the shattering of his illusions about his wife and his precious health have freed him and made him happier. If he does become a spark, his wit will stand him in good stead: anyone who can refer to Lady Knowell as "Madam Romance, that walking library of profane books" (II.i), is not merely a comic butt.

In addition to good construction, dialogue, and characterization, the play offers the audience a number of appeals to eye and ear. The bedroom scene (IV.iv), in which Lucia tries to get Wittmore out unseen by the drunken and amorous Sir Patient, is almost pure farce and certainly pure fun. Sir Credulous finishes a cacophonous serenade, the staging of which involves a long street and "a pageant of an elephant coming from the farther end, with Sir Credulous on it" (III.ix). His country love song and his battle with the alderman's servants led by the canting Abel add the final comic touches to a scene that must have exploited all the resources of the Restoration stage. With the Bettertons, Smith, Mrs. Currer, Anne Quin,[10] Anthony Leigh (Sir Patient) and James Nokes (Sir Credulous) to lead the exceptional cast, it is no wonder that the play was a distinguished success. Indeed, Leigh and Nokes were so famous in their roles that the play is said to have died with them in 1692, for no adequate replacements could be found.

The success of *The Rover*, at first published anonymously, led Mrs. Behn to put her name on the title page of the third issue, but she seems still to have been the object of attack by critics. This prefatory address, for example, justifies her haste in printing on the ground that she needed to defend herself against criticism that the play was bawdy and its author a plagiarist. She attributes the attack to resentment of a woman dramatist, and she is probably right: either charge could have been made against almost any playwright of the period. The epilogue presents her case again, this time in witty couplets.

She might well have omitted both prefatory address and epilogue; the excellence of the play was her best defense.

V   The Feigned Courtesans

More than a year elapsed between the production of *Sir Patient Fancy* and *The Feigned Courtesans; or, a Night's Intrigue* (Dorset Garden, March 1679).[11] The prologue complains of the way in which real "plots," like that of Titus Oates, have drawn attention from the stage:

> The devil take this cursed plotting age,
> 'T has ruined all our plots upon the stage.
> Suspicions, new elections, jealousies,
> Fresh informations, new discoveries,
> Do so employ the busy fearful town,
> Our honest calling here is useless grown. . . .

This statement and the fulsome dedication to Nell Gwyn imply that Mrs. Behn was having more difficulty than in previous years; the dedication may have been a necessary lapse in taste.

Mr. Summers says that the play, "if not Mrs. Behn's masterpiece (a title it disputes with *The Rover*, Part I, and *The Lucky Chance*), at least is one of the very best and wittiest of her sparkling comedies" (II, 304); but it is difficult to understand his judgment, even though Downes and other early writers agree with him.

The play is primarily intrigue comedy with a considerable infusion of farce: the intrigue involves Marcella and Cornelia, who have come to Rome disguised as expensive prostitutes to escape Marcella's forced marriage with Octavio and Cornelia's seclusion in a convent. Marcella loves Sir Harry Fillamour, whom she has met at Viterbo; Cornelia soon loves Galliard. Julio, brother of the two girls, has been contracted to Laura Lucretia, Octavio's sister, while away on the Continent; arriving secretly, he joins Galliard in pursuing La Silvianetta (Cornelia). Laura Lucretia loves Galliard; but, in passing herself off as Silvianetta, she mistakenly lures Julio instead.

After enormously complicated and often confusing intrigue, in which the disguised girls assume the further disguise of boys, and all the men get confused in one dark scene after another, the stratagems are unraveled: Laura must be content with Julio, Octavio resigns Marcella to Sir Harry, and Cornelia talks Galliard into marriage.

The low comedy plot concerns Sir Signal Buffon and his tutor, the Reverend Timothy Tickletext. Led on by Petro, who assumes four different disguises, they both separately pursue Silvianetta, producing more confusion and a great deal of farcical business. Unlike *Sir Patient Fancy*, *The Feigned Courtesans* offers very little comedy of wit. As a pair of witty lovers, Cornelia and Galliard resemble Hellena and Willmore in *The Rover*, as the following passage shows:

CORNELIA.
Faith, stranger, I must consider first, she's skillful in the merchandise of hearts, and has dealt in love with so good success hitherto, she may lose on venture, and never miss it in her stock. But this is my first, and should it prove to be a bad bargain, I were undone for ever.

GALLIARD.
I dare secure the goods sound—

CORNELIA.
"And I believe will not lie long upon my hands."

GALLIARD.
Faith, that's according as you'll dispose on't, Madam. For let me tell you—gad, a good, handsome, proper fellow is as staple a commodity as any's in the nation. . . .   (III.i)

These dialogues are among Mrs. Behn's best, but there are few of them. Instead, the audience is regaled with the farcical antics of Sir Signal and Tickletext. Occasionally the antics are genuinely funny, as when Petro, posing as a civility-master, cons the two out of their jewelry and money (II.i), or when Tickletext is used by his creator to satirize English chauvinism: "St. Peter's church, Sir? You may as well call it St. Peter's hall, Sir: It has neither pew, pulpit, desk, steeple, nor ring of bells, and call you this a church, Sir? No, Sir, I'll say that for little England, and a fig for't, for churches, easy pulpits—[Sir Signal *speaks:* And sleeping pews.]—they are as well ordered as any churches in Christendom; and finer rings of bells, Sir, I am sure were never heard" (I.ii). But when the two are used with several of the major characters merely to complicate an intrigue situation, comedy disappears into farce; and Mrs. Behn wastes some of her most promising material.

The epilogue again suggests that the very popular farce was emphasized to insure the play's success:

> So hard the times are, and so thin the town,
> Though but one playhouse, that must too lie down;
> And when we fail, what will the poets do?
> They live by us as we are kept by you. . . .

It is interesting to note in this connection that the farcical scenes have very little intrinsic relation to the rest of the play. Ned Blunt is used as a balancing element in the structure of *The Rover;* Tickletext and Sir Signal have no such thematic function here.

The farce, Petro's disguise, the numerous duels, two songs, and endless intrigue managed with sure professional skill, must have sufficiently amused the audience to insure the play's success. And Mrs. Behn was fortunate in her actors. Tony Leigh played Petro, Nokes and Underhill acted Sir Signal and Tickletext; these three would have carried off the farce brilliantly. Smith played Fillamour; Betterton, Galliard; Elizabeth Currer, Marcella; and Elizabeth Barry, Cornelia. The play did not become part of the repertoire, but it was acted more than once after the opening run, and was revived for at least five performances in the 1716-17 season.[12]

VI The Young King

Following the judgment of Summers, Woodcock and others put *The Young King* before *The Feigned Courtesans,* and assign both plays to the spring of 1679.[13] *The Young King* was probably produced, however, in September or October of that year. The epilogue refers to "his Royal Highness's second exile into Flanders"; James had returned from Belgium in August, 1679, but had gone back on September 25 for nearly a month before going on to Scotland. The discrepancy is not significant for the study of Mrs. Behn's dramatic career, for in its original form *The Young King* obviously belongs among her early plays. The

[58]

dedication "To Philaster"[14] refers to it as "this youthful sally of
my pen, this first essay of my infant poetry," and internal evidence confirms at least the first half of the statement. Summers
and Woodcock accept the last part as well, and so do most other
writers on the play. According to Summers, the earliest sketch
was written

whilst she was still a young girl at Surinam. Upon her return to
England the rhyming play had made its appearance, and . . . she
turned to her early MS. and proceeded to put her work, founded
on one of the most famous of the heroic romances, into the fashionable couplets. . . . Whilst she was busy, however, *The Rehearsal* . . .
gave a severe blow to the drama it parodied. Accordingly, Mrs.
Behn . . . put her tragicomedy on one side until the first irresistible
influence of Buckingham's burlesque had waned ever so slightly, and
then, . . . after subjecting *The Young King* to a thorough revision, . . .
she had it produced. . . ." (II, 103-04).

Hargreaves (p. 175) also accepts a Surinam version, though
he rightly considers the Orsames plot the original basis of
the play.
    This view requires a play first written at Surinam in some
unspecified medium—blank verse or prose—then rewritten in
couplets, then rewritten a third time in a mixture of blank verse
and prose, but so clumsily that several traces of the couplet
version remain. There is no substantial evidence to support
any of this as theory, much less as fact. The dedication does
mention that the author's "virgin muse" has measured "three
thousand leagues of spacious ocean" and "visited many and
distant shores," but nothing in it clearly associates the writing
of any specific part of the play with any specific place, or even
with the period of traveling. In fact, while the grammatical
antecedent of *muse* is "this youthful sally of my pen," the lines
which follow may refer to the author rather than to her work:
the prose of the period was not always sensitive to the resulting
ambiguity.
    Again, the author's presence in Surinam at some point is now
highly probable; but, since no one yet knows Mrs. Behn's
maiden name or date of birth, it is difficult to decide even so
germane a question as her age at the time of her visit. She
may have written a full draft there, but she may equally well

have written a sketch or a scene, and finished it after her return
to England. And there are couplets in the play, though aside
from two speeches (I.ii and IV.iii), most of them come at the
end of scenes and are thus quite conventional. But there are
also numerous couplets in *The Forced Marriage* and *The Amorous Prince,* and no one has yet suggested that these plays
underwent translation from the heroic mode.

In fact, the mixture of prose, rough blank verse, mediocre
couplets, and more than adequate prose is typical of Mrs. Behn's
early style. The presence of the couplets may well be a bow
to the popularity of heroic drama, but this is a reasonable inference: Summers rejects Edmund Gosse's suggestion that the
delay in production was due to the author's failure to get the
work accepted until she became an established dramatist, but
this suggestion is equally plausible, and far simpler than
Summers' own.

Whatever the cause of the delay in production, *The Young
King* was an anachronism in 1679. It belongs to the school of
romantic tragicomedy she had by then abandoned except for
such themes as the happiness of the pastoral life and the evil
of forced marriages. The main plot, derived from La Calprenède's *Cléopatra,* combines a pastoral theme in a Beaumont
and Fletcher setting with the usual measure of disguises, mistaken identities, masques, and fighting; but intrigue as such is
much less prominent than romance.

In the action, Theresander, prince of Scythia, assumes the
role of Clemanthis to woo the Dacian princess Cleomena. Since
the two countries are at war, his two identities involve him
in considerable difficulties. Obliged by lot to fight a duel with
himself, he dresses his friend Amintas as Clemanthis; but, before
the duel can take place, Amintas is left for dead by assassins
hired by Artabazes, one of his rivals for Cleomena. Cleomena,
believing Thersander has killed her lover, disguises herself as a
shepherdess and stabs him. Both he and Amintas recover, the
latter with the aid of a Druid priest; the complications are unraveled, and Thersander and Cleomena unite the two countries
by their marriage. Amintas is rewarded with his faithful Urania,
who had followed him to prison in Dacia; his Dacian counterpart Vallentio receives Cleomena's attendant Semeris for his
services to the princess.

The second plot, derived from Calderon, is a variant of an old folk tale.[15] To thwart an oracle, Orsames, prince of Dacia, has been imprisoned from infancy in an island castle, and seen only by his tutor Geron. He is accidentally exposed, first to Urania, then to others; and, for political reasons, he is given a trial reign of a night. He behaves badly, and is returned to his prison convinced by Geron that the whole affair was a dream like his "vision" of Urania. He remains discontented, so Vallentio, at Cleomena's request, secures him the army and the citizenry, and they set him upon the throne. The oracle is lamely explained away as having been fulfilled by the one night's reign, and Orsames marries his first cousin Olympia, the woman he is most attracted to.

The two plots have no inherent relation to each other, and very little nominal connection. The one-night reign (II.i) does not involve any of the main characters: Orsames is Cleomena's brother, but they meet only at the end of the play; he sees Amintas and Urania briefly in one scene. The final scene cannot hope to fuse credibly two plots so separated throughout their course; as a result, one tends to think of them as belonging to different plays. Unity of construction is further shattered by Mrs. Behn's comic treatment of Orsames in most scenes; this not only makes unconvincing his change to kingly status at the end but also jars with the romantic plot, which is as serious as the conventions of tragicomedy allow.

Mrs. Behn's skill is evident only in the conduct of the Thersander-Cleomena plot, which is very well put together; for the rest, an audience must be content with a few good things in every act. Lyces' speech on constancy (I.i) is an example:

> 'Tis grown the fashion now to be forsworn;
> Oaths are like garlands made of finest flowers,
> Wither as soon as finished;
> They change their loves as often as their scrips,
> And lay their mistresses aside like ribbons
> Which they themselves have sullied.

The pastoral fallacy produces a number of pleasant lines, such as Cleomena's "How much more charming are the works of nature / Than the productions of laborious art!" (I.ii); so do some of the discussions between Orsames and Geron. The elaborate stage effects provided for Orsames' first reign would make a fine show, and there are the usual songs and masked dancing. The play also offers in the two brief appearances of the mob of citizens (IV.vi and V.iii) its only real comedy and its best success. Mrs. Behn exposes the mob satirically, but portrays it vividly and accurately: they want a king because they haven't had one and because they need a figurehead on whom to vent their anger when a battle is lost.

But such isolated bits cannot redeem a poor play, and it is not surprising that there is no account of any performance. Summers argues that it is "far better than the rank and file Restoration tragicomedy," and that "since two editions were published we may safely assert its popularity" (II, 104). But these are dubious recommendations; the best evidence that *The Young King* was Mrs. Behn's first play is its inferiority to both *The Forced Marriage* and *The Amorous Prince*.

VII   The Second Part of the Rover

The Second Part of the Rover, produced around January of 1681 at Dorset Garden,[16] was also quarried from Killigrew's *Thomaso,* and obviously attempts to capitalize on an earlier success. The inimitable Willmore reappears in pursuit of the beautiful courtesan La Nuche, his Hellena having died at sea. Joining him in Madrid are the officers Shift and Hunt, and the comic squires Ned Blunt and Nicholas Fetherfool. Belvile is missing; his place is filled by Beaumond, the nephew of the English ambassador; he, and also old Don Carlo, are Willmore's rivals. Beaumond is engaged to Ariadne, who pursues the Rover through most of the play, adopting the "breeches" disguise of a young man when convenient.

After a very complicated set of intrigues, involving as usual mistakes in the dark, duels, and spirited dialogue, Ariadne is content to marry Beaumond after all; and La Nuche throws prudence to the winds and accepts the impoverished Willmore as her lover. The comic plot presents Willmore in the disguise of a mountebank. Aided by Shift and Hunt, he thwarts the efforts of Blunt and Fetherfool to marry a giantess and a dwarf, respectively, for their money; cozening the comic figures throughout the play, Willmore delivers the "monsters" to his brother officers instead. As in *The Feigned Courtesans,* the characters in the comic plot, especially Fetherfool, participate in part of the main plot and add an element of farce to the mistakes and duels.

Given the amazing amount of complication conventional in the comedy of intrigue, *The Second Part of the Rover* is very carefully constructed. Since Beaumond is no Belvile, Willmore emerges clearly as the central figure in the play, a role symbolized by his mounting the bench in Act II.ii to dispense magical potions to most of the other characters. His disguise becomes thematically significant in the light of their need to be deceived—to ignore the realities of their respective situations. Since he is in the sequel the same frank and cavalier gallant he was in Part I, his masking demonstrates dramatically the sham of conventional society:

WILLMORE.

Come, buy this coward's comfort, quickly buy. What fop would be abused, mimicked, and scorned, for fear of wounds can be so easily cured? Who is't would bear the insolence and pride of domineering great men, proud officers, or magistrates? Or who would cringe to statesmen out of fear? What cully would be cuckolded? What foolish heir undone by cheating gamesters? What lord would be lampooned? What poet fear the malice of his satirical brother, or atheist fear to fight for fear of death? Come, buy my coward's comfort, quickly buy. (II.i)

Beaumond, Don Carlo, and to some extent Fetherfool are not so much foils to Willmore as representatives of another view of love that is opposed to his. Don Carlo embodies the empty lust of the old, and Fetherfool mere appetite which any woman will serve: both are the butt of jokes, and no one takes them seriously. Beaumond is the real antagonist, for he has not only youth and health but also money and position. He does not love La Nuche as much as Willmore does, and she does not love him at all. But he can pay for her favors, and Willmore cannot. This contrast of values, which determines much of the main action, is of course present also in Part I: Ariadne and La Nuche are Hellena and Angelica reborn, and Beaumond is an amalgam of Antonio and Pedro. But in Part II the conflict between the two value systems is more sharply drawn, and more is made of it. In fact, Act V, scene i presents its culmination almost as an abstract tableau, with Love contending with Interest for Beauty:

BEAUMOND.

    I yield him many charms: he's nobly born,
    Has wit, youth, courage, all that takes the heart;
    And only wants what pleases women's vanity,
    Estate: the only good that I can boast,
    And that I sacrifice to buy thy smiles.

LA NUCHE.

    See, Sir—here's a much fairer chapman—(*To* Willmore.)—You may be gone.

WILLMORE.

    Faith, and so there is, child, for me; I carry all about me, and that, by heaven, is thine: I'll settle all upon thee but my sword, and that will buy us bread. I've two led horses, too; one thou shalt manage, and follow me through dangers.

LA NUCHE.

    A very hopeful, comfortable life! No, I was made for better exercises.

WILLMORE.

    Why, everything in its turn, child, but a man's but a man.

BEAUMOND.

    No more, but if thou valuest her, leave her to ease and plenty.

WILLMORE.

    Leave her to love, my dear: one hour of right down love,
    Is worth an age of living dully on.
    What is't to be adorned and shine with gold,
    Dressed like a god, but never know the pleasure?
    No, no, I have much finer things in store for thee.

                                     Hugs her.

LA NUCHE.

    What shall I do?
    Here's powerful Interest prostrate at my feet,
                       Pointing to Beaumond.

> Glory, and all that vanity can boast;
> But there (*To* Willmore.), Love unadorned, no covering
>   but his wings. . . .   (V.i)

In Part I, the Rover accepts Hellena's price, and the ending
compromises wish-fulfillment with the demands of reality. In
this play, the ending fulfills the wish for love free from restraint,
for love as intense as it is ephemeral. The two lovers here are
no Arthur Donnithorne and Hetty Sorrel in the wood, acting
in adolescent ignorance: La Nuche accepts Willmore's philosophy, though her own servant Petronella embodies the inevitable consequences of such decisions.

The weakness of *The Second Part* lies not in the management of the main intrigue—which is in some respects better
than, and equally as plausible as, that in the earlier play—but
in the distraction caused by the farce. In Part I, Blunt is the
only comic character, and his cozening does not bulk large in
the play. Here he is joined by Fetherfool, who largely replaces
him as the butt of Mrs. Behn's satire on country squires. So
much is reasonable. But he is also joined by Harlequin, Scaramouch, a giantess, and a dwarf; and the shift to slapstick tends
always to destroy the effect of the main plot. The dialogue
about marriage between Beaumond and Ariadne (II.ii) is pure
comedy of manners; the visit of Ned and Nicholas to the monsters, pure farce. Mrs. Behn had shown in several earlier plays
that manners comedy could be integrated with some success
into an intrigue plot, but she fails entirely to convince one that
the two scenes above belong in the same play. The farce, the
numerous songs, the pageant and dance in the mountebank scene,
the elaborate stage directions—all these contribute variety and
insure an interesting spectacle; and Mrs. Behn is an expert in
them all. But they are not subservient to the central idea, and
it is this which accounts for the inferiority of the sequel.

In the first production, Mrs. Barry added La Nuche to her
many roles; Betty Currer played Ariadne; Smith recreated Willmore; Underhill and Nokes acted Blunt and Fetherfool. But
though much better than most sequels, the play suffered their
usual fate, and was never so popular as Part I. The fulsome
dedication to James (then Duke of York) might have got the

author the customary gratuity, but it could not preserve her work on the boards.

VIII The False Count

The False Count, Mrs. Behn's next play, reveals a change of pace. It is a light and breezy comedy, very close to pure farce though not slapstick, and thoroughly delightful. The writer of the epilogue refers to it as "a slight farce, five days brought forth with ease, / So very foolish that it needs must please," and suggests that it will suit its audience well:

> For though each day good judges take offence,
> And satire arms in comedy's defence,
> You are still true to your jack-pudding sense.
> No buffoonry can miss your approbation;
> You love it as you do a new French fashion.
> Thus in true hate of sense, and wit's despite,
> Bant'ring and shamming is your dear delight. . . .

If the author was writing down to her audience's taste, she nevertheless succeeded in creating very good entertainment.

The plot, unlike those of her intrigue comedies, is slight; in this case she borrows the main action from A. Montfleury's *Ecole des jaloux.* Don Carlos, the governor of Cadiz, is betrothed to Julia, who has been forced to marry Francisco, a jealous old merchant now come to Cadiz with his wife, her sister Clara, and Isabella, his daughter by a former marriage. Isabella is to marry Antonio; Clara, Don Carlos. But Isabella, a proud and conceited girl, will have nothing to do with a mere merchant; and Antonio is already in love with Clara. Don Carlos and Antonio, aided by the former's servant Guzman, arrange an elaborate trick to gain their ends. They hire Guiliom, a witty chimney-sweep, to impersonate a count and to court Isabella. While the entire party is aboard a rented boat in the harbor, it is "attacked" by a "Turkish" ship; and all are taken to Antonio's country villa, which Francisco and Isabella believe to be the Sultan's harem. There the old merchant, under threat of death, resigns his wife to Don Carlos, who poses as the Sultan. The trick is exposed by the arrival of the fathers of Julia and Antonio, but too late: Francisco cheerfully resigns Julia to Don Carlos, Clara and Antonio are safely married, and

Isabella must take the now-revealed chimney-sweep as her husband of quality.

Don Carlos, Antonio, Julia, and Clara are sketched well enough to provide a basis for the comedy, but never really developed. Attention focuses on the comic characters—Francisco, Guzman, Guiliom, Julia's maid Jacinta—and on the amusing scenes produced by the trick. Francisco is allied with all the other rich old merchants cuckolded in Mrs. Behn's plays; but, like the best of them, he is individualized as well. His speeches reveal jealousy as his ruling "humor," but his language is full of specific rhythms and phrases that distinguish him from, say, Sir Timothy Tawdrey:

FRANCISCO.
Not you, Sir? Why, look ye, your young governor who now is, made most desperate love to her who is now my wife, d'ye mind me? But you, being a man of an exact judgment, to her great grief, gave her to me, who best deserved her, both for my civil behavior, and comely personage, d'ye understand me? But now this Carlos, by his father's death being made governor, d'ye see, is to marry your other daughter Clara, and to exasperate me, would never let me be at quiet till he had got both of us hither to Cadiz, to grace his wedding. A pox of his invitation! Was I so civil to invite him to mine? (I.ii)

His terror before Don Carlos the Sultan and his comical resignation of Julia's virtue to save himself are matched in the Isabella plot by the antics of "the most renowned Don Gulielmo Roderigo de Chimneysweeperio," whose story owes much to Molière's *Les précieuses ridicules.* His sooty hands and occupational metaphors would betray his origin to anyone but the snobbish Isabella:

Oh! I am doubly wounded, first with her harmonious eyes,
Who've fired my heart to that degree,
No chimney ever burnt like me.
Fair lady, suffer the broom of my affection to sweep
All other lovers from your heart. (III.ii)

It is not surprising that the audience liked the play: the unity of tone and the excellence of the banter would have guaranteed its appeal even if the audience knew the major sources in Molière and Montfleury. Smith played Don Carlos in the original production, put on at the Dorset Garden Theatre late in November or early in December, 1681.[17] The great comedian Nokes played Francisco; Underhill and Lee took the parts of Guzman and Guiliom, respectively; and Betty Currer acted Isabella. The play was presented often during the period, though it was not a standard repertory piece; it was revived during the 1715-16 season, and again in 1718 and 1730.[18]

IX   The Roundheads

The Roundheads; or, The Good Old Cause (1681) has been mentioned in Chapter One as Mrs. Behn's major contribution to the political strife occasioned by the Oates plot, the Exclusion Bill, and the machinations of Monmouth and Shaftesbury. The play, based on John Tatham's *The Rump*, proceeds by farcical exaggeration; Lambert, Fleetwood, Lord Wariston, Duckenfield, and several other prominent figures involved in the events of 1659-60 are not only comic analogues to the chief Whig politicians but also mere buffoons and cowards. Lambert schemes against Fleetwood for power, hoping to be king; Wariston supports first one and then the other, depending on who pays more; and Duckenfield is concerned only with his stable. The council meets only to wrangle, cant, and vote one another pensions; in one scene (IV.iii) they all get drunk and engage in a cushion dance, reeling about the great Chamber of State. General Monk's announced arrival puts an end to their machinations; rumps are roasted in the streets of London in anticipation of Charles's arrival, while Wariston and Hewson disguise themselves as ballad singer and country dancer in an unsuccessful effort to escape retribution.

To this crude satire is joined one of Mrs. Behn's typical love intrigues. Freeman loves Lady Desbro, wife of an old canting Cromwellian whom she has married only to scheme for her lover's sequestered estate. Freeman's friend and fellow-royalist Loveless falls in love with the would-be queen, Lady Lambert. Both pursue their amours in the midst of the political farce, and both of course conclude them successfully, aided by the opportune death of Desbro from fright and the imprisonment of Lambert. Further comedy is furnished by Ananias Goggle, a prurient lay elder who embodies Roundhead hypocrisy and cant.

Woodcock calls the play indecent, "a ridiculous and unjustifiable lampoon."[19] But it is restrained in comparison with its model, and certainly far less offensive than many contemporary political satires. To judge its exaggeration against historical fact, as Woodcock and others do, is not entirely to the point; for *The Roundheads* is not serious political drama but farcical propaganda. As farce, parts of it are quite funny; for example, the first appearance of the oligarchy (I.ii), and the excellent scene in which the council vote one another pensions and places (III.i). The lecherous Goggle is a fine comic creation, and Mrs. Behn's mob of apprentices is realistically and amusingly presented.

The play fails, not because of bias or historical untruth, but because it is poorly conceived and clumsily constructed. The mixture of love intrigue with farce seriously mars Part II of *The Rover;* here, where the force is not only dominant but political, the mixture is intolerable. In the midst of Loveless' gallantry to Lady Lambert, for example, he breaks into a long, ridiculous eulogy of Charles that is occasioned by the quite gratuitous presence of the crown and scepter in Lady Lambert's boudoir. Again, Lady Lambert's pretensions to grandeur and place are satirized in scene after scene; but in the love intrigue she must be a suitable heroine for romantic comedy, and the two roles are obviously inconsistent. Finally, some scenes in the play have no structural *raison d'être*. Loveless, in one such, disguises himself as a woman to attend a meeting of the Ladies' Grievance Committee; the scene satirizes the Puritans, to be sure, but has no connection whatever with either the political plot or the love intrigue.

X The City Heiress

Though one of Mrs. Behn's worst plays, *The Roundheads* was apparently successful on the stage.[20] Yet its author seems to have realized that politics and her special talents could be more harmoniously integrated, for her next play is not only better satire but far better art. *The City Heiress; or, Sir Timothy Treat-all*, produced at Dorset Garden in late April or early May, 1682,[21] is one of her best comedies. It opens with Sir Timothy Treat-all disinheriting his nephew Tom Wilding for being a spendthrift and a Tory, despite the protests of Tom's

friend Sir Charles Meriwill. Tom, the Rover of the play, is pursuing both Lady Galliard, a rich widow, and Charlot Get-all, a
young heiress.

To revenge himself on his uncle, Tom introduces his mistress
Diana to Sir Timothy as Charlot; and the old miser pursues her
vigorously. Charlot, meanwhile, disguises herself to keep an
eye on Tom. Sir Charles's uncle Sir Anthony has admired Tom's
style all along, and, in scenes indebted to Philip Massinger's
The Guardian, spurs his nephew to more aggressive courtship.
Eventually, the young knight tricks the widow into marriage,
but not before she has yielded to Tom. Sir Timothy entertains
the company at his marriage, and is visited by a foreign "nobleman" who offers him the crown of Poland; in the night, however, Tom and his accomplices tie up the household and steal
his uncle's money and documents. The scene, borrowed from
Thomas Middleton's *A Mad World My Masters*, is very well
integrated: the plunder gives Tom his independence, and after
admitting his Polish masquerade, he marries Charlot. Sir Timothy is left with Diana, and since the stolen documents are
treasonable, he is effectively silenced.

In general, the satire helps to establish the dramatic character Sir Timothy as well as to hit at Shaftesbury. Whiggism and
avarice are common characteristics of the old city merchants who
figure prominently in most of Mrs. Behn's comedies, and Sir
Timothy is simply a more telling variation. To anyone familiar
with the history of the period, the political satire adds a second
dimension to the play; but the comedy also stands on its own
merits.

The play is carefully constructed. As is her wont, Mrs. Behn
uses two lovers, Tom and Charles; though their aims overlap,
they deepen the play by providing contrast. Tom is the wild
gallant with two intrigues afoot and a mistress at home. Charles
is more like Belvile in *The Rover*: conservative, true to one
pursuit, importunate only after prodding by his frisky uncle.
The pair of lovers is balanced by Lady Galliard and Charlot;
the former is the romantic heroine, the latter the young and
saucy wit Mrs. Behn made famous in Hellena. As usual, the
young are set against the old. Tom and his associates Fop-
pington and Dresswell outwit Sir Timothy, and young Diana

craftily secures by marriage all that is left. The contrast between their gaiety and vitality and the dullness and vices of
Sir Timothy is heightened by the characterization of Sir Anthony Meriwill. He is near Sir Timothy's age, but loves life
and its pleasures as much as Tom. The very sight of Lady Galliard puts "small Cupids at hot-cockles" in his heart (I.i), and
his no-nonsense pushing of Charles at Lady Galliard forms an
interesting contrast to Sir Timothy's rather lecherous and greedy
wooing of Diana. This careful structuring has not gone unnoticed. Hargreaves, whose analysis of the play is very good, says
that "the pattern of action, plot, and dialogue, together with
musical background, are unequaled in the period for their utilization of visual and aural elements, and should clearly be
called artistry rather than craftsmanship" (p. 212).

Though the political satire runs throughout the play, the tone
is established primarily by the comedy of wit. The dialogue is
fast-paced and witty. Less polished and ironic than the best of
Congreve or Wycherly, Mrs. Behn's language is nevertheless
racy, suited to the characters, full of the rhythms of speech,
and, above all, plain and natural. When characters use artificial
or conventional words they are either marked out for fops, or
fail to gain their ends, as in the scene in which the backward,
polite Charles woos Lady Galliard:

LADY GALLIARD.
  Please you sit, Sir.

SIR CHARLES.
  Madam, I beg your pardon for my rudeness.

LADY GALLIARD.
  Still whining?   *Dressing her self carelessly.*

SIR ANTHONY.
  D'ye hear that, Sirrah? Oh, damn it, beg pardon! The rogue's
quite out of's part!

SIR CHARLES.
  Madam, I fear my visit is unseasonable.

SIR ANTHONY.
  Unseasonable! Damned rogue! Unseasonable—to a widow! Quite
out!

LADY GALLIARD.

There are indeed some ladies that would be angry at an untimely visit, before they've put on their best faces, but I am none of those that would be fair in spite of nature, Sir. (*To* Closet.)—Put on this jewel here.

SIR CHARLES.

That beauty needs no ornament: heaven has been too bountiful.

SIR ANTHONY (*aside, vexed*).

Heaven! Oh Lord, heaven! A Puritanical rogue; he courts her like her chaplain!

LADY GALLIARD.

You are still so full of university compliments—

SIR ANTHONY.

D'ye hear that, Sirrah?—Ay, so he is, so he is indeed, Madam. (*Aside to him.*)—To her like a man, ye knave!

SIR CHARLES.

Ah, Madam, I am come—

SIR ANTHONY.

To show yourself a coxcomb.

LADY GALLIARD.

To tire me with discourses of your passion.—(*Looking in the Glass.*) Fie, how this curl sits!   (II.iii)

Later in the play, he acts a gallant's part and wins the lady.

The scenes between Tom and Lady Galliard echo themes from previous plays: freedom versus convention, youth and health versus age and security, love versus money, loving versus marrying. In *The City Heiress,* as in *The Rover,* the gallant is tamed after he has his fling. Charlot's youth, beauty, wit, and money gild the husband's cage; but, as with most of Mrs. Behn's young rakes, one suspects that Wilding will never really give up his role as the unattached lover forever in pursuit:

DRESSWELL.

Pox on 'em all! Prithee, turn out those petty tyrants of thy heart, and fit it for a monarch: love, dear Wilding, of which thou never knew'st the pleasure yet, or not above a day.

[72]

WILDING.
　Not knew the pleasure! Death, the very essence, the first draughts
of love! Ah, how pleasant 'tis to drink when a man's a dry! The rest
is all but dully sipping on.　　　　　　　　　　　　　　　　　(II.ii)

The original production must have been first-rate. Nokes
played Sir Timothy; Betterton, Tom Wilding; and Lee, Sir Anthony. Elizabeth Barry acted Lady Galliard; Mrs. Butler, Charlot; and Elizabeth Currer, Diana. The political appeal and the
strong cast made the play initially popular, but the topical satire
probably determined its life; it was played at intervals for some
years, revived for at least one performance in 1707, but then
disappeared from the boards.

XI　Like Father, Like Son

Between *The Roundheads* and *The City Heiress* appeared the
only known Aphra Behn play never to have been printed.[22]
The title, *Like Father, Like Son; or, The Mistaken Brothers*,
is known from the prologue, which was printed in 1682. The
epilogue, printed on the verso, refers to several of the actors in
the company, and calls the play a comedy, not a political play:
"No Salamancan doctorship's abused, / Nor a malicious statesman here accused." It is supposed to have been an adaptation
of Thomas Randolph's *The Jealous Lovers*, but its failure was
apparently complete since a play had to be pretty poor fare
to escape publication.
　Whether her arrest in August, 1682, frightened her from the
stage, whether she was kept from it by her opponents or by the
managers, or whether she could no longer make a profit from
her plays, Mrs. Behn produced nothing of which we have record before 1684,[23] and no more plays until the spring of 1686.
The politically-slanted plays therefore mark the end of the
middle period of her career. By any standard it was a productive time: between July, 1676, and May, 1682, she had produced eleven known plays, and possibly three others—some
fourteen full-length works in fewer than six years.

CHAPTER 4

The Dramatist: Late, Posthumous, and Doubtful Plays

I *Late Plays*

THE LUCKY CHANCE

WHEN Mrs. Behn returned to the theater she had published a volume of fictional love letters, a book of poems, a miscellany, some translations, and one or two panegyrics. One of the letters mentioned in Chapter One,[1] written on August 1, 1685, refers to "the playing my first play" as an event not far off; and *The Lucky Chance; or, An Alderman's Bargain,* was indeed produced at the Theatre Royal in Drury Lane about April, 1686.[2]

The play, as Mrs. Behn notes in the preface, is "a comedy of intrigue"; but she follows her customary procedure in making intrigue a framework for a good deal of wit and the usual touch of farce. As in most of her comedies, there are two sets of heroes and heroines and, this time, two old knights as well. Before the play begins, Bellmour has been exiled for killing a man in a duel. He returns to London only to find from his friend Gayman that his fiancée Leticia believes him dead and is about to marry Sir Feeble Fainwould. Gayman has spent all his money on his mistress Julia, now married to Sir Cautious Fulbank, and is living disguised in Alsatia, the underworld area of London. Bellmour disguises himself as Sir Feeble's nephew; that night, while helping his "uncle" undress, he discovers that the old man holds his official pardon. At the same time, he prevents the consummation of Sir Feeble's marriage by sending him to Sir Cautious about a pretended plot.

Meanwhile, Julia finds out Gayman's disguise from Sir Cautious' prentice. She steals a bag of gold from her husband and sends the prentice Bredwell, disguised as a devil, to deliver it to Gayman with an invitation to a mysterious assignation. The disguise, together with songs and a pastoral dance, half convinces Gayman that he is confronted with black magic, and he comes to Julia believing her a hag. Their amours are interrupted by the arrival of Sir Feeble; but, while each of the old men wonders what is wrong with the other, Bredwell and Gayman exit as ghosts. Sir Feeble returns home barely in time to prevent Leticia's elopement with Bellmour. The next day, Gayman gambles with Sir Cautious for a night with Julia, and wins. In the evening, Bellmour again thwarts Sir Feeble—this time by posing as his own ghost—and elopes with Leticia to Sir Cautious' house. The banker, meanwhile, pays his debt by conducting Gayman to Julia. She discovers the old man's substitution of Gayman for himself, and resigns her husband's bed in revenge. The two lovers gain their mistresses, and Bredwell is rewarded with Sir Feeble's daughter Diana, formerly contracted to the fop Bearjest.

There is little falling off in this play from Mrs. Behn's best work, and some scenes in the play are masterpieces of contrivance. For example, Gayman in Act II talks his Alsatian landlady into pawning her daughter's caudle cup in a scene full of realistic dialogue and broad humor. Sir Feeble and Sir Cautious are worthy additions to the long list of city dotards Mrs. Behn dissects in a dozen plays; and the scene in which they sit gaping at each other in mutual astonishment, each thinking the other mad, is one of her best:

SIR FEEBLE.
Well, Sir, do you not know that I am married, Sir? And this my wedding night?

SIR CAUTIOUS.
Very good, Sir.

SIR FEEBLE.
And that I long to be in bed?

SIR CAUTIOUS.
Very well, Sir—

SIR FEEBLE.
Very good, Sir, and very well, Sir! Why then, what the devil do I make here, Sir? *Rises in a rage.*

SIR CAUTIOUS.

Patience, brother, and forward—

SIR FEEBLE.

Forward? Lend me your hand, good brother, let's feel your pulse. How has this night gone with you?

SIR CAUTIOUS.

Ha, ha, ha, this is the oddest conundrum! Sure he's mad! And yet, now I think on't, I have not slept tonight, nor shall I ever sleep again till I have found the villain that robbed me. *Weeps.*

SIR FEEBLE (*aside*).

So, now he weeps. Far gone! This laughing and weeping is a very bad sign! —Come, let me lead you to your bed.

SIR CAUTIOUS (*aside*).

Mad, stark mad! —No, now I'm up 'tis no matter; pray ease your troubled mind. I am your friend. Out with it! What, was it acted? Or but designed?

SIR FEEBLE.

How, Sir? (III.iv)

Finally, the gambling scene and its aftermath, in which greed and reputation (not love, of course) contend in the soul of old Sir Cautious, not only point up the cupidity and cold self-love of the class he represents, but also provide a superb contrast to Gayman's warm and free affection.

Gayman, one of the last of Mrs. Behn's rovers, is matched well with the witty and mature Julia; Bellmour's constancy once more rings the changes on Belvile. The gallant wins his mistress, the faithful lover his bride; convention is both flouted and accepted, but in both cases love and youth, as always, prevail over hard cash and age. Some of the scenes between Gayman and Julia, and between Sir Cautious and his lady (e.g., V.iv) are vehicles for the comedy of wit; so is the contrast between the stupid, foppish Bearjest and the polished Bellmour and Gayman. The farcical scenes, particularly that in which Bearjest is saddled with Julia's maid Pert, contribute very little to the play, nor does the elaborate pageant which precedes Gayman's nocturnal visit to his unknown benefactor. But these are relatively minor flaws in a play remarkable for good craftsmanship, brisk and comic dialogue, varied action, and sustained characterization. The well-constructed intrigue plot is without the confusion of incident and disguise which mars such plays as *The Feigned Courtesans* and *The Younger Brother*.

In the first production, Leigh and Nokes acted Sir Feeble and Sir Cautious; Betterton, Gayman; Tom Jevon, Bearjest; and Mrs. Barry, Lady Fulbank. The play had a successful run, though Fields in the summer of 1718, and was adapted by Hannah attacked by some critics for indecency; and it was played at intervals for some ten years. It was revived at Lincoln's Inn Cowley in 1786 as *A School for Greybeards*.

THE EMPEROR OF THE MOON

The Spectator for March 26, 1711, prints a letter from one William Screne, a disappointed actor who has never had a line to speak in his career but who is "one of the men in the hangings in the *Emperor of the Moon*." The allusion is to Act II, scene iii of Mrs. Behn's farce, produced at Dorset Garden in March, 1687, by the United Company.[3] The play is a remarkable one, combining a love intrigue, satire on contemporary foibles, the antics of the *commedia dell' arte*, and the spectacle of a contemporary opera, into one integrated whole.

The intrigue plot is slight. Elaria and Bellemante, daughter and niece to Doctor Baliardo, love Cinthio and Charmante. Baliardo denies the girls their lovers, reserving them for the lunar beings his astrological studies assure him exist. The two men, aided by Harlequin and Scaramouch, eventually convince the doctor they are the King of the Moon and Prince Thunderland, wed their ladies before the masquerade is discovered, and cause Baliardo to give up his lunar fantasies.

The *commedia dell' arte* is interwoven by having Scaramouch be Baliardo's servant and Harlequin Cinthio's and by having the two contend for the affection of Mopsophil, the young ladies' duenna. This device assures the unity of the piece; there is only one brief scene (III.i) in which the antics of the servants are not fused with the romantic plot. The importance of Harlequin and Scaramouch in the action establishes *The Emperor of the Moon* as a farce in the "new" style, drawn from Italian and French models; parts of half a dozen scenes, in fact, come from *Arlequin empereur dans la lune,* a contemporary example. Mrs. Behn had already produced a "traditional" farce in *The False Count,* and she had introduced the two pantomime figures into *The Second Part of the Rover.* In that play they were external to the action and therefore weakening; in this play she fully assimilates them, and the result is one of the finest plays of its type in English.

Act II, scene iii perhaps best shows the delicate blending of farce, fantasy, pageantry, and romance which inspires the play. The ladies enter in elaborate costumes, and the dialogue briefly touches the comedy of manners:

ELARIA.

If he be a man of honor, cousin, when a maid protests her innocence—

BELLEMANTE.

Ay, but he's a man of wit too, cousin, and knows when women protest most, they likely lie most.

Soon the two lovers, also in masquerade, come in with Harlequin, Scaramouch, and musicians; after a brief dialogue, they watch an antic dance, listen to a pastoral duet accompanied by flute and harpsichord, and engage in a dance themselves. When Baliardo returns unexpectedly, Scaramouch poses them all as figures in an elaborate tapestry sent as a gift to the doctor; they are discovered only by the antics of Harlequin, who hits Baliardo every time he approaches to inspect the "allegory." When Baliardo returns with pistols, Scaramouch pretends the whole episode is a magically acted out dream of his. Elaria and Bellemante then pretend to have been visited in a dream by the lunar potentates, and with their help Scaramouch convinces the doctor that his hopes for a lunar alliance are to be fulfilled.

The lightness and gaiety which permeate all three acts are considerably enhanced by the theatrical effects Mrs. Behn creates. The final scene calls upon every resource of the contemporary stage, combining an elaborate masque, the traditional mock combat between Harlequin and Scaramouch, and the return of the whole fantasy to the every day world. Set in a "gallery richly adorned with scenes and lights," it opens with a pageant, described thus in the stage directions: "The scene in the front draws off, and shows the hill of Parnassus; a noble large walk of trees leading to it, with eight or ten Negroes upon pedestals, ranged on each side of the walks. Next Kepler and Galileo descend on each side, opposite to each other, in chariots, with perspectives in their hands, as viewing the machine of the zodiac. Soft music plays still."

Kepler talks briefly to Baliardo, and the company then watches the zodiac descend to music. "When it is landed, it delivers the twelve signs. Then the song, the persons of the zodiac being the singers. After which, the Negroes dance and mingle in the chorus." The song is an ode reminiscent in tone and structure of Dryden's *Secular Masque*, with a fine chorus:

> For since love wore his darts
> And virgins grew coy,
> Since these wounded hearts,
> And those could destroy,
> There ne'er was more cause for your triumphs and joy.

Such pageantry, which suggests contemporary operatic spectacles, has been prepared for carefully earlier in the play: the extravagance and sumptuousness are necessary to maintain Baliardo's delusion. The climax soon follows: "After which, the globe of the moon appears, first like a new moon. As it moves forward it increases, till it comes to the full. When it is descended, it opens, and shows the emperor and the prince. They come forth with all their train, the flutes playing a symphony before him, which prepares the song. Which ended, the dancers mingle as before." The emperor and prince appear in a chariot "made like a half moon" and, after a dance by the whole train, wed the two girls. To provide the anti-climax, Harlequin and his rival, dressed as great heroes, descend in chariots and "fight at barriers" for their lady.

The scene and the play are superbly ended when the victorious Scaramouch doffs his helmet and is recognized by Baliardo. The masquers are his friends; the lunar powers, Cinthio and Charmante. A Prospero in reverse, Baliardo has been the victim rather than the creator of his supposedly magical universe. When these revels end, the pageant leaves more than a wrack behind. For the doctor burns his astrological books and invites the company to celebrate his "happy recantation." To himself he says gravely,

I see there's nothing in philosophy.
Of all that writ, he was the wisest bard, who spoke this mighty truth:

> "He that knew all that ever learning writ,
> Knew only this—that he knew nothing yet."

The play was a great success on the stage. Underhill took the part of Baliardo; Tony Leigh, of Scaramouch. Thomas Jevon was an admirable Harlequin, and Pinkethman was outstanding as his successor. More than one hundred and thirty performances are recorded between 1687 and 1749.[4] In fact, *The Emperor of the Moon* was not only Mrs. Behn's last successful play but also her longest lived: after many years as a repertory piece, and numerous revivals, it was acted (with some alteration) for the last time in 1777.[5]

II *Posthumously Produced Plays*

THE WIDOW RANTER

George Jenkins staged the best of Mrs. Behn's two posthumous plays, *The Widow Ranter; or, The History of Bacon in Virginia*, at Drury Lane in November, 1689.[6] Its major source, an eight-page quarto pamphlet entitled *Strange News from Virginia; Being a Full and True Account of the Life and Death of Nathanael Bacon Esquire* . . . had appeared in 1677. Had Mrs. Behn written her play soon thereafter, she would surely have been able to produce it during the period of her greatest popularity. Since she did not, since the Indian king and queen in the play are somewhat similar to those in her novel *Oronooko*, published in 1688, and since both the play and the novel satirize colonial officials, it is reasonable to suggest a date of composition near 1688.

The title page of *The Widow Ranter* calls it a tragicomedy, probably for want of a better term since this description is inaccurate. The "tragic" plot concerns Bacon's Rebellion, an historical event which took place in Virginia in 1675-76. The real Bacon, an enigmatic figure, was an English gentleman who had emigrated to the colony about 1673 and was elected General by the colonists soon after. His commission was delayed by the governor, and Bacon was called a traitor for attacking the Indians before he received it. His popularity forced the governor to yield until he had additional troops; in the meantime, Bacon won another victory against the Indians. When the governor's troops arrived, Bacon defeated them, burned Jamestown, then died suddenly in 1676.

Mrs. Behn follows her source roughly in describing Bacon and the situation, but she replaces the governor with a council composed largely of comic cowards, and involves her hero in an heroic romance with Queen Semernia, a virtuous Indian. She also has him commit suicide after accidentally killing Semernia; he dies, ironically, just as his forces win the victory. Bacon is interesting even thus changed, but the discrepancy between the haughty and ambitious man confronting the corrupt council and the conventional lover of heroic tragedy confronting the conventionally noble and virtuous Indian queen is too great to be dramatically credible. The one posture belongs to realism; the other to romance.

Bacon himself figures in less than a quarter of the play, though the rebellion provides its foundation. The rest of the action is taken up with three other plots. The first concerns the gallants Friendly and Hazard, who intrigue for Chrisante Downright and Madam Surelove, respectively, and who win them honorably as the play closes. Both serve with the forces against Bacon, and Friendly has a supposed rival in Bacon's subordinate Daring; these are their only connections with the "main" plot. The second plot is built around the scoundrels Dullman, Brag, Timorous Cornet, Whimsey, Whiff, and Boozer, especially the last four. In scene after scene the buffoons display their cowardice, fair-weather loyalty, and drunkenness. While they are primarily comic figures, they are also vehicles of the author's satire on the qualities of colonial administrators. The final plot gives the play its title: the widow Ranter, wealthy, outspoken, and punch-loving, pursues and finally wins Daring.

Woodcock calls *The Widow Ranter* "in every way . . . one of Aphra Behn's best plays,"[7] but such a judgment is difficult to understand. The play, as printed, lacks unity both of structure and of tone. The tragic part does end tragically; and, though Bacon's death, like Hamlet's, signals the healing of civil strife and the establishment of a better society, this merely confirms the essential seriousness of the action. However, the intrigue plot is totally irrelevant thematically to the Bacon story; and although the widow's wooing can be seen as a useful comic contrast to the two gallants', little use is made of the possibility. Again, the cowardly justices typify the social order against which Bacon struggles, but they have no significant relationship to the pair of lovers or the widow. Mrs. Behn is after everything at once: history, tragedy, heroic romance, intrigue, farce, and satire. The materials are there; she makes an attempt to dovetail all the actions required; but the task is impossible. The wonder is that one can follow such an unfocused narrative.

Jenkins' production was apparently a failure, and no other performances are recorded. The cast was not especially distinguished, though Underhill played Timorous and Anne Bracegirdle, Semernia; the only remarkable achievement was Elizabeth Currer's as the widow. Jenkins ascribes the failure to miscasting and to the butchering of scenes. Miscasting there certainly was, since the deformed Sanford acted the part of Daring. Some cuts were also certainly made: the courtroom scene (III.i), which is good farcical satire, was omitted, although it was restored in the printed version; the ghost of the Indian king, perhaps fortunately, was cut in both. It would be easy to confuse the play intolerably by injudicious cuts, poor casting, and poor acting. The finest circumstances, on the other hand, could hardly have assured such an amalgam a very long life.

THE YOUNGER BROTHER

The failure of *The Widow Ranter* probably delayed the production of *The Younger Brother; or, The Amorous Jilt*, Mrs. Behn's other posthumous play. Gildon finally put it on at Drury Lane about February, 1696,[8] after altering the first act to remove "that old bustle about Whig and Tory (which was the subject of most of the second scene)" and place "the character of a rake-hell in its room" ([A3]); he also made a number of cuts that were restored in the printed version. The reference to party controversy suggests a date in the early 1680's for part of the play; superficial resemblances to the novel *Hattigé,* by Sébastien Brémond (translated 1680), and a borrowing in Act IV from Tom D'Urfey's *The Royalist* (1682), support the suggestion. Most of it is probably later: in *Oronooko* (1688) Mrs. Behn mentions "Colonel Martin, a man of great gallantry and goodness, and whom I have celebrated in a character of my new comedy by his own name . . ." (pp. 209-10). This can only refer to George Marteen, the younger brother who gives the play its title.

Whatever the date of composition, the intrigue comedy badly needed a more thorough reworking than Gildon gave it. Like *The Widow Ranter,* it suffers from too many plots and too little focus. In one strand George Marteen, passing with most people as the gallant Lejere but with his father as a sober young man, pursues four different objectives. He wants to revenge himself on Mirtilla for jilting him, to replace his rake-hellish brother Sir Merlin as heir to his father's estate, to marry his father's fiancée Teresia rather than the ancient Lady Youthly, and to reveal Mirtilla's true character to his friend Prince Frederick, who has fallen in love with her.

In another strand, George's sister Olivia, disguised as Mirtilla's page, is pursued by her mistress while herself pursuing Wellborn. Olivia and Wellborn are contracted but have never met; Wellborn, in several scenes dressed as the prince to cause further complications, also pursues her. A final strand, though a weak one, involves the carousing of Sir Merlin and his foolish friend Sir Morgan Blunder, to whom Mirtilla is married. After considerable intrigue, George gains all his objectives and is married to Teresia. Wellborn marries Olivia, the prince gives Mirtilla to her husband, and Lady Youthly must be content with her young chaplain Mr. Twang. Sir Rowland is happy at everything, even Sir Merlin's marriage to a cast-off mistress.

George is Mrs. Behn's last rover, while Olivia and Teresia share some of the wit and pluckiness of Hellena. Mirtilla, however, is unlike any other character in the plays: beautiful, amorous, and cynical, she laughs at George's attempts at revenge, yet voluntarily confesses her duplicity to the prince. These characters are well developed, their dialogues are usually spirited, and Mrs. Behn occasionally touches levels of satire deeper than in any other play. Mirtilla, for example, is a kind of Becky Sharp, heartless and amoral; yet in her career she uses and exposes the hypocrisy of her society:

GEORGE.
Thou own'st the conquest, then?

MIRTILLA.
With as much vanity as thou wouldst do, if thou hadst won his sword. Hast thou took care wisely to teach me all the arts of life, and dost thou now upbraid my industry? Look round the world, and thou shalt see, Lejere, ambition still supplies the place of love. The worn-out lady that can serve your interest, you swear has beauties that outcharms fifteen; and for the vanity of quality, you feign and languish, lie, protest, and flatter. All things in nature cheat, or else are cheated.

GEORGE.
Well said; take off thy veil, and show the jilt.   (IV.i)

The other characters are less interesting. The prince, an impossible fool romantically blind to all but love, is a cardboard character who belongs in a particularly vapid tragicomedy. Sir Merlin and Sir Morgan, who have a great many lines, add nothing to the plot except mediocre farce. Wellborn, Lady Youthly, and Sir Rowland are hardly more than able sketches.

The first part of the play, less dominated by the prince and the antics of Sir Merlin and Sir Blunder, is better than the rest. Toward the end Mrs. Behn's usual control of detail weakens. Olivia, for example, is supposedly witty and clever, but twice bungles the unmasking of Mirtilla. The appearance of Sir Merlin's bride is totally unprepared for, while the conduct of Mirtilla and the prince at the end of the play does not square with their characters as earlier presented. Gildon may be partially right in ascribing the play's failure on the boards "to some faction that was made against it" ([A3]), but its inherent weaknesses would in any case have precluded continued success. One concludes that Mrs. Behn, in leaving both *The Widow*

Ranter and *The Younger Brother* among her papers, was wiser than her literary executors.

III *Plays Attributed to Mrs. Behn*

THE WOMAN TURNED BULLY

In addition to the seventeen extant plays known to be by Mrs. Behn, at least four others have been attributed to her. They are *The Woman Turned Bully* (1675), *The Debauchee; or, The Credulous Cuckold* (1677), *The Counterfeit Bridegroom; or, The Defeated Widow* (1677), and *The Revenge; or, A Match in Newgate* (1680). Of the first, Summers says, "She has also been given *The Woman Turn'd Bully*, a capital comedy with some clever characterization, which was produced at Dorset Garden in June, 1675 . . ." (I, xxxvii). Although Summers admits there is no evidence to support the claim, Woodcock seems to accept the attribution (pp. 119). Hargreaves, whose analysis of these attributions is one of the strengths of his dissertation, dismisses the claim in a note (p. 250) stating that the play is not as much like Mrs. Behn's work as these critics suggest. Without evidence, the ascription must be rejected.

THE DEBAUCHEE

On the other hand, Mrs. Behn has been widely credited with *The Debauchee* although Gerard Langbaine says merely that it is ascribed to her "by some."[9] Produced at the Duke's Theatre in February, 1677,[10] it is an alteration of Richard Brome's *Mad Couple Well Matched*. The plot of the later version differs in only minor respects from its original: the adaptation adds a scene which is merely summarized in Brome (III.i), deletes two minor characters who do not appear until Act V of the *Mad Couple*, and has Loveless rather than Bellamy (a lady in disguise) as Careless' rival for the rich widow. Since Brome's play is so little changed, the case for Mrs. Behn's authorship must rest on rather thin evidence. One would like to think that the deletion of unnecessary characters at the end is evidence of her craftsmanship, but if she adapted *The Revenge*, she added an entirely irrelevant scene at the end of that play. The only structural alteration which supports her case is the substitution of Loveless for Bellamy. Mrs. Behn tends, in her intrigue comedies, to establish two sets of lovers who are often rivals at first; the change brings *The Debauchee* closer to that pattern.

Aside from plot, a further consideration is important: the adaptor tones down crudeness, roughness, and bawdy throughout, both in characters and in language. Brome's Careless, for example, is rawer, blunter, and less sensitive than his counterpart in *The Debauchee;* and Brome's Wat suggests a trade in Act I scene i which the later play silently omits. The language of the scene between Bellamy (Clara) and the lascivious Mrs. Saleware (end of Act III) is considerably refined in the adaptation; in fact, this restrained handling of the older play's diction is the most striking difference between the two pieces, and represents the supposedly immoral Mrs. Behn's practice in every adaptation she is known to have made.

The only change which is atypical of Mrs. Behn is the added scene (III.i) in which Careless comes home drunk and engages the butler Sim in an alcoholic conversation. The scene is unlike any in Mrs. Behn's known work, and it is most unhelpful in smoothing down and lightening the character of Careless. If the play is hers, one must assume she made the change because she objected to too much reported action.

If the internal evidence for Mrs. Behn's authorship is meager, the external evidence is more so. The date fits a period in which she is known to have made other adaptations—*The Rover,* for example. All of her plays between 1676 and 1682 were produced at Dorset Garden; so was this one. *The Debauchee* is the only play listed in a bookseller's advertisement printed in the first edition of *The Rover*.[11] Finally, the absence of another strong contender for the authorship is a negative point in her favor. Hargreaves argues that the positive evidence "tends to prove" the adaptation was done by Mrs. Behn (p. 260). Both external and internal evidence, taken together, make it probable that the play is hers; further than this, one cannot reasonably go.

THE COUNTERFEIT BRIDEGROOM

The Counterfeit Bridegroom, produced in the fall of 1677 at the Duke's Theatre, was attributed to Mrs. Behn by John

Genest; later historians ascribe it either to her or to Thomas Betterton.[12] Like *The Debauchee*, it is an adaptation of an earlier play, in this case Middleton's *No Wit, No Help like a Woman's*. In this intrigue comedy, Peter Santloe has secretly married Clarina; his friend Sanders loves Eugenia. For a while it seems that Clarina may be Peter's long-lost sister, but eventually Eugenia turns out to have been substituted for Clarina when both were babies, and the two sets of lovers are united. The underplot concerns the efforts of Mrs. Hadland and her husband to get back their estate from the widow Landwell, whose many suitors include Mrs. Hadland's brother Noble. Eventually, the Hadlands get their own, and Noble gets the widow.

The adaptation is far more extensive in this instance than in *The Debauchee*. Middleton's play is very long, diffuse, and mostly in verse. The later play shortens the text almost by half, considerably tightens it structurally, and turns it into prose. Several scenes in Middleton's play are omitted entirely, and many more are drastically reduced and rearranged. The underplot in Middleton bulks very large and involves considerable low humor and farce; in *The Counterfeit Bridegroom*, it is clearly subservient to the main action and more closely related to it. The later play reduces considerably the astrological imagery of Middleton (one of the widow's suitors is Mr. Weatherwise), and cleans up much of the earlier playwright's bawdy. The diction generally is smoothed out and made more contemporary. Both the widow's fool and a Dutch merchant who figures in the Peter-Clarina plot are omitted. Finally, the supposed incest between Philip and Grace (Peter and Clarina) has existed for several months in Middleton's version; in the later play their marriage is not consummated until the true identity of Clarina is revealed.

The Counterfeit Bridegroom is in almost every respect a better play than its original; if Aphra Behn rewrote it, she made it as much her own work as she did *The Rover*. The combination of intrigue and farce in the older play was just the kind of thing at which she excelled; *No Wit, No Help* was far more congenial to her talents than Brome's comedy. There were already two sets of lovers, for example, and a sub-plot with opportunities for both complicated action and spectacle. The adaptation thus looks more like an Aphra Behn comedy to begin with than does *The Debauchee*, the numerous changes permit more thorough comparison with her known work, and the comparison strongly suggests her authorship.

The craftsmanship required to make such thorough revision and rearrangement of scenes is very great, and craftsmanship is one of Mrs. Behn's outstanding characteristics as a dramatist. The rapid pace, natural dialogue, and realistic prose are also typical of her work, as in the gayer tone of the adaptation. Only one touch is atypical: the weakening of Eugenia's role as secondary heroine. Mrs. Behn would normally tend to add to, rather than subtract from, such a part. All in all, the external evidence is about the same as for *The Debauchee:* time and place are suitable and possible. Although Hargreaves is almost certainly correct in arguing that Thomas Betterton's known plays at this period are very different from *The Counterfeit Bridgroom*,[13] the conclusion must again be indefinite: Mrs. Behn's authorship is probable, but not beyond doubt.

THE REVENGE

The last of the doubtful plays is *The Revenge*, produced about June, 1680, also at the Duke's Theatre.[14] An adaptation of John Marston's *The Dutch Courtesan*, it is attributed to Betterton in the Wing Catalogue but to Aphra Behn by both Langbaine and Genest. Montague Summers, who claims for the authoress both *The Debauchee* and *The Counterfeit Bridegroom*, says merely that "Betterton's adaptation . . . has sometimes been erroneously ascribed to Mrs. Behn by careless writers" (I, xxxvii). Hargreaves, after a thorough analysis, concludes that she was the author (p. 284).

The play is a thorough reworking of Marston's. The plot is altered, but the outlines are similar. Wellman, a typical gallant, is leaving his mistress Corina for his fiancée Marinda. His companion Friendly loves Marinda's sister Diana, and he reproves Wellman's amours only to fall in love with Corina on sight. The deserted mistress pretends she will accept his love if he kills Wellman, and the two friends agree to fake a fatal duel. Wellman intends, however, to teach Friendly a lesson;

and, when the latter is arrested for "murder," Wellman comes to his rescue at the last possible minute. The plot ends with the two sets of lovers ready to marry and with Corina satisfied with Sir John Empty, Diana's rejected suitor. The underplot is farcical and involves the stratagems used by Trickwell to cheat the vintner Dashit and his wife in revenge for their having taken his estate. Their quarrel, very thinly connected with the main action, is resolved equitably by Wellman at the end of the play.

Most of the changes found in the later play follow a familiar pattern. Poetry is changed to prose, the diction is refined and brought up to date, bawdy is excised or reduced, and two minor characters are combined into one. Two further alterations are even more significant. In Marston's play, Malheureux (Friendly) fades out of the play after Wellman reveals himself; Diana's suitors are the blunt Tissefeu and the prating Caqueteur (Sir John Empty and Mr. Shatter). The adaptation turns Friendly into Diana's lover and adds to his role; instead of having Sir John marry Diana, as in Marston, he is furnished with Wellman's cast-off mistress. The change strongly suggests the double set of lovers familiar in so many Aphra Behn plays.

The other alteration is equally revealing. Francischina (Corina) in Marston's play is more a whore than a mistress; she speaks a coarse language full of broken "Dutch," and even responds to Trickwell's advances. In the end she is hauled off to the severest punishment Newgate affords. *The Revenge*, on the other hand, presents her as an English girl seduced only by Wellman, refines her sentiments as well as her diction, has her motivated entirely by revenge on Wellman, and recognizes the justice of her cause by providing her with a well-off if foppish husband in Sir John Empty. The changes align her in some respects with Angelica Bianca and La Nuche[15] and turn her from a crude blend of passion and vulgarity into a serious study in character.

Again, only one scene seems unlike Mrs. Behn. In Act V occurs a Newgate prison scene full of crude realism, in which Shamock berates other condemned felons for ineffective begging; on the eve of his own execution he shows them how to do it properly. His wife has confessed a crime she did not commit merely to die with him, and in part of the scene they inspect their common coffin while Trickwell picks their pockets. The scene is interesting and shows the same mastery of Hogarthian detail evident in the dialogue of Betty Flauntit in *The Town Fop*, the Alsatian scene in *The Lucky Chance*, and the touches of vulgar realism in *The Widow Ranter*. But it is wholly irrelevant to the rest of the play, and such a lapse in craftsmanship is difficult to explain.

On July 6, 1680, Narcissus Luttrell, whose habit of buying and dating items soon after their publication has often been helpful to scholars, purchased a copy of *The Revenge*, entering the date, the price, and also the name of the author: "Mrs. Ann Behn." William Van Lennep, who first noticed this copy, remarked that although most writers follow Baker's *Biographia Dramatica* in assigning the play to Betterton, "Luttrell's note upon the author, made at the time the play appeared in print, is strong evidence that Langbaine was correct."[16] This additional bit of external evidence, added to the characteristic alterations of the original, make the ascription of *The Revenge* to Mrs. Behn as near a certainty as one can get in dealing with an anonymous play.

CHAPTER 5

The Dramatist: Sources

ORIGINAL plays in the Restoration are not so common as modern attitudes toward plagiarism and imitation might suggest. Dramatists felt free to make use of older plays for plots, characters, and incidents; they felt even freer about borrowing material from foreign authors or from non-dramatic literature. Audiences, if they recognized the source of a play, did not seem to mind; and only when wholesale borrowing without acknowledgment occurred did most early historians complain. In fact, though Gerard Langbaine lists many of Mrs. Behn's sources, his introductory comment is generous:

> Most of her comedies have had the good fortune to please: and though it must be confessed that she borrowed very much . . . yet it may be said in her behalf, that she has often been forced to it through haste: and has borrowed from others' stores, rather of choice than for want of a fund of wit of her own: it having been formerly her unhappiness to be necessitated to write for bread. . . . 'Tis also to her commendation, that whatever she borrows she improves for the better. . . .[1]

Mrs. Behn is typical of her period in this practice as in many other respects. Only two of her plays, *The Forced Marriage* and *The Feigned Courtesans,* are entirely original.[2] Three others make minor use of sources. The scenes in *The Lucky Chance* in which Pert leads Gayman to Lady Fulbank's bed and she teases him about it later (III.iv and IV.i) are borrowed from James Shirley's *The Lady of Pleasure* (IV.i and V.i). Even here, where she borrows the outline of the action and some dozen speeches, Mrs. Behn contributes much of the detail—the masque, for example. Olivia's plight in Act IV, scenes i and ii of *The Younger Brother* is drawn from the similar predicament of Philippa in Tom D'Urfey's *The Royalist* (1682), although Mrs. Behn handles the situation differently. Also, the heroine of her play bears some resemblance to that of Sébastien Brémond's *Hattigé,* a popular *roman à clef* translated in 1680. Mirtilla, however, is no Lady Castlemaine, and the plots of the two works are quite dissimilar.

The Widow Ranter uses its source pamphlet only for the character of Bacon and the general situation; for Summers' statement that except for the catastrophe and the Indian queen plot "she keeps fairly closely to her sources" (IV, 218) is misleading. A dozen details can be traced to *Strange News. . . ,* but they are used in an original manner in the play. For example, the pamphlet mentions a Parson Clough who discovered Bacon at a house in Jamestown and who noticed the general's men lining the bushes as if in ambush. In *The Widow Ranter,* Clough becomes Parson Dunce, a fairly important character in the comic plot; and the ambush is set against Bacon by the cowardly members of the council.

Those plays in which Mrs. Behn makes fairly extensive use of source material constitute a second group. There are seven of them, belonging to all stages of her career: *The Amorous Prince, The Dutch Lover, Sir Patient Fancy, The Young King, The False Count, The City Heiress* and *The Emperor of the Moon.* Three of this group borrow primarily from fictional originals. As Gerard Langbaine was quick to note, *The Dutch Lover* is based on an anonymous romance called *The History of Don Fenise, a New Romance Written in Spanish by Francisco de Las Coveras, and Now Englished by a Person of Honor* (1651). Most of the play comes from the stories in this work of *Enfamie and Teodore, Don Jame,* and *Frederic;* but Mrs. Behn considerably alters the original, combining characters and amalgamating plots into something very different from the novel. English drama from Beaumont and Fletcher's *A King and No King* through Ford's *'Tis Pity She's a Whore* shows the popularity of the incest theme; both the novel and Mrs. Behn's play belong to this tradition.

The main action of *The Young King* is based on Part VIII of La Calprenède's interminable romance *Cléopatre,* as translated into English by Robert Loveday in 1668. The Cleomenes-Thersander plot follows the original fairly closely, but Mrs.

Behn considerably shortens the time of the action by having parts of the narrative summarized. She also creates an under-plot by saving the wounded Amintas and providing him with the faithful Urania. The Orsames plot, which gives the play its title, is indebted to Calderon's philosophical play *La Vida es Sueño*, although Mrs. Behn makes her king into a comic figure.[3] The scene in which Orsames has his trial reign is closest to the original; little of Calderon remains in the rest.

The Amorous Prince also borrows from both fiction and drama. The titular plot, involving Frederick, Laura, Curtius, and Cloris, is apparently original. The secondary plot, in which Antonio insists that his friend Alberto test his wife's fidelity, comes from Cervantes' *Don Quixote*, with minor details from an earlier play on the same subject, Robert Davenport's *The City Nightcap*. The main debt is to the novel; but the happy endings and the complications added with Ismena and her disguise make even this action at least half Mrs. Behn's own work. From Davenport's play she seems to have gotten the names of Antonio and Lorenzo, and the idea of the country bumpkin Guiliom. Even here she makes several changes: Lorenzo in *The City Nightcap* is Abstemia's husband; Philippo, his friend; and Antonio, a prince who tries three times for Abstemia before revealing his identity and unraveling the complications of the plot. In *The Amorous Prince*, Lorenzo becomes a fop; Antonio, the husband of Clarina; and Alberto, the friend. The whole action involving Davenport's Antonio is omitted. Since all of the major plot, nearly half of the secondary, and the dialogue, songs, and other stage effects are original, the total borrowing in this play is considerably less than at first appears.

The remaining plays in this group are indebted to earlier drama. To the contemporary criticism that *Sir Patient Fancy* "was made out of at least four French plays" Mrs. Behn ingenuously replied in her preface "To the Reader" that she "had but a very bare hint from one, the *Malade imaginaire*, which was given me translated by a gentleman infinitely to advantage." Actually, Sir Patient's hypochondria, part of the Wittmore-Fancy and Lodwick-Isabella actions, and a number of minor details are adapted from Molière's play. Mrs. Behn also borrows parts of Act V from *L'amour médecin*.[4] As D. H. Miles notes, "The adaptation as a whole is ingeniously managed to produce a comedy of intrigue. There is not much paraphrase."[5] The first entrance of Sir Credulous and Curry, in which the foolish knight laments the loss of his horse, is borrowed from the first appearance of Sir Amphilus and Trebasco in Richard Brome's *The Damoiselle*, Act II, scene i, though Mrs. Behn alters the dialogue extensively. Other resemblances between the two knights are superficial; Mrs. Behn alters and surpasses Brome's characterization, and she gives her country baronet a much greater part in her comedy.

The False Count also borrows from Molière. The humbling of proud Isabella by Guiliom the chimney-sweep owes much to *Les précieuses ridicules,* though the only point of direct paraphrase is the moment in Act III, scene ii when Guiliom (Mascarille) offers to show the ladies a wound in his "back parts." Summers demonstrated in 1930 Mrs. Behn's debt to Antoine Montfleury's *Ecole des jaloux* for her main plot.[6] Francisco and Julia are his Santillane and Léonor; Don Carlos keeps his name as well as his position as governor of Cadiz; Guzman is hardly altered from Gusman. Mrs. Behn, however, has made numerous changes. Clara and Antonio are added to provide contrast to Don Carlos and Julia. The two sets of lovers are then used to combine the two plots, since Isabella is intended for Antonio and Clara for Don Carlos. In Montfleury, Gusman is the Grand Turk; in Mrs. Behn's play his master plays this role and is Julia's current, not her former, lover.

The City Heiress borrows from two Jacobean plays, Philip Massinger's *The Guardian* and Thomas Middleton's *A Mad World My Masters.* Sir Anthony Meriwill and his nephew Sir Charles are taken from Durazzo and his ward Caldoro in Massinger's play, even to details of the dialogue, especially in the first two acts. Wilding owes something to Caldoro's rival Adorio, at least at first, although only Mrs. Behn's gallant wins a night with the lady. The conduct of the intrigue is quite different in the two plays, and so is the tone: the comedy of manners element bulks large in Mrs. Behn's play but is, of course, missing in Massinger's. From Middleton come a few hints for the character of Sir Timothy Treat-all, and the fine comic robbery in Act V scene i. Wilding and Dresswell are Middleton's Folly-wit and Maweworme in this scene; some dialogue is also borrowed. The two plays together account for perhaps a sixth of *The City Heiress*, certainly not more.

The best discussion of the background of *The Emperor of the Moon* is that of Leo Hughes and A. H. Scouten.[7] The play's source is the *commedia dell' arte* play *Arlequin empereur dans la lune* (1684); Mrs. Behn seems to have seen "the piece performed often enough to retain the substance of the six or eight scenes from which she borrowed." They include the action in the tickling scene (end of I.ii), parts of the scene in which Harlequin caps Bellemante's verses and the two lovers hide in the closet (I.iii), and "rough parallels and piece-meal borrowings" in the cart scene (III.i), the apothecary scene (III.ii), and the final scene (III.iii). Hughes and Scouten also believe that the tapestry scene (II.iii) may owe something to Nolant de Fatouville's *Arlequin Jason ou la toison d'or*. At least half the scenes and much of the detail and dialogue in many of the borrowed scenes are original. The use of the romantic plot to give structural unity to an otherwise miscellaneous collection of farce and pantomime is also original and assures the artistic superiority of the play to its source.[8] The operatic quality of the pageantry is a final addition, one barely suggested in the *commedia*.

Those of Mrs. Behn's plays which adapt, rather than borrow from, an earlier drama make up a final group. It includes *The Town Fop*, both parts of *The Rover*, *Abdelazer*, and *The Roundheads*.[9] Her practice in such instances was to take from the older play the basic situation, the central characters, and some details of action and language. Her alterations are always extensive, especially those affecting structure and dialogue; and in every case, the result is a better play than the source.

The Town Fop is based on a popular old play by George Wilkins, entitled *The Miseries of Enforced Marriage*. Lord Plotwell is taken from Lord Falconbridge, guardian of Scarborrow (Bellmour). He uses his power to force Scarborrow to marry his niece Katherine (Diana), though Scarborrow has solemnly contracted himself to Sir John Harcope's daughter Clare (Celinda). Wilkins also has his hero send a letter reporting his marriage. Clare returns one saying that she is dead, but, in the older play she then kills herself. Scarborrow's debauches are, appropriately, longer and deeper than Bellmour's; the tavern in-

terview between Bellmour and Charles (Thomas and John Scarborrow) condenses several scenes in Wilkins. Mrs. Behn also
uses a severely cut version of the elaborate intrigue by which
Butler (Trusty) marries Scarborrow's younger sister (Phillis)
to Sir Francis Ilford (Sir Timothy). The only other borrowings
of importance involve a brief dialogue between Scarborrow and
Clare, which Mrs. Behn has between Sir Timothy and Celinda
at their first meeting, and Sir Francis Ilford's two hangers-on,
Bartley and Wentloe, who provide a few hints for Sham and
Sharp.

The differences between the two plays are far more remarkable than plot comparisons can suggest. Wilkins' play—a crude,
moralistic melodrama—combines soap-operatic tragedy with
coarse and vulgar comedy; its language is stilted, clumsy, and
endlessly sententious. The whole intent is expressed in the title;
but, after asserting throughout the play that living with Katherine is sin and whoredom, and ruining his brothers and sister
as well as himself by his profligate existence, Scarborrow suddenly is relieved of both scruple and poverty by the fortuitous
deathbed repentance of the wicked old guardian. Then, as if
nothing has happened, he quickly embraces his wife, children,
siblings, and eight thousand pounds a year.

The contrast between this play and the superbly constructed
comedy of manners Mrs. Behn makes of it is astonishing. The
crudity, the melodramatic morality, and the clumsy language
vanish. Friendlove is added to provide a strong pair of secondary lovers; Bellmour's uncle and guardian are combined into
one milder Lord Loveless; Sir Timothy is made genuinely comic,
not merely a disgusting leech. The fine comedy of Betty
Flauntit and Driver is added, and both tragedy and brutality
are omitted. Cuts are made in the interest of tight structure
and convincing characterization, and the action is restricted to
London.

The source of *Abdelazer* is *Lust's Dominion; or, The Lascivious Queen,* a play wrongly ascribed on its title page to Christopher Marlowe. On the whole, the adaptation is close to the
original. Mrs. Behn does drop King Philip; Alvero, the old
father of Alonzo; the king of Portugal; and the two crudely
comic friars. And she adds Roderigo as a minion of the Moor,
and Isabella's maid Elvira. But despite her cuts, she follows

the first two acts rather faithfully, preserving much dialogue as well as action and characterization. The last three acts are altered: scenes are rearranged, the handling of Florella's death is different, Isabella is killed rather than imprisoned to repent, and Abdelazer is made regent rather than king.

Most of Mrs. Behn's changes are improvements. For example, in *Lust's Dominion* Philip kills Osmin in cold blood and Abdelazer when he is helpless; she has Abdelazer kill Osmin and die fighting. In the older play, the cardinal's defection to Abdelazer is poorly motivated, and he at first admits publicly to being Philip's father; in *Abdelazer,* the defection is based on Mendozo's attraction to Isabella, and he denies the paternity charge from the beginning. The omission of the friars Crab and Cole is a final important improvement: their vulgar comedy and wretched murder detracts from the tragic quality of the main action. As these examples suggest, Mrs. Behn worked successfully to make a better play than she found: in structure and in psychology *Abdelazer* is sound. But such revision of language as she made is inadequate to charge the play with significance, and more was probably beyond her powers. It is interesting to note that Edward Young's version (*The Revenge,* 1721) is no better.

Both parts of *The Rover* are founded on *Thomaso; or, The Wanderer,* a ten-act comedy by Thomas Killigrew published in 1664. The two parts drew Gerard Langbaine's only real condemnation: he thought Killigrew's comedy excellent, and Mrs. Behn's ingenuous postscript disturbed him: ". . . notwithstanding her apology in the postscript to the first part; I cannot acquit her of prevarication, since Angelica is not 'the only stolen object,' as she calls it: she having borrowed largely throughout. The truth is, the better to disguise her theft, she has . . . fleaed the eel by beginning at the tail; yet notwithstanding, what she has omitted of worth in her first part, she has taken into the second; and therefore could not justly call these plays her own."[10]

Langbaine is right in part. Despite the postscript, almost all of the characters and most of the action in both parts are taken from *Thomaso.* But one reading of Killigrew's play will convince anyone that Mrs. Behn was nevertheless justified in calling *The Rover* hers. *Thomaso* presents its reader with seventy-three scenes in ten acts. It is liberally sprinkled with speeches that take up a third or a half of a folio page. Its plots are expanded in scene after scene, and little attempt is made to keep any one of them dominant throughout, or to maintain suspense. The dialogue is often cumbersome, with massive polished sentences and long paragraphs. *The Rover,* on the other hand, is a fast-paced and eminently actable comedy that is clearly dominated by a single action.

Detailed comparison of the two plays shows Mrs. Behn's essential originality. Willmore resembles Killigrew's Thomaso in his gallantry and outrageous fondness for amorous adventure. But Thomaso is presented throughout as really loving Serulina, and he eventually undergoes a change of character: "The wanderer shall in this friendship [love for Serulina] prove he has in all his past flames but practised how to love."[11] His roving is rather lamely explained as due to pride—to his not wishing to be rejected as a poor Cavalier. Serulina, whom he marries at the end, is just adventuresome enough to appear in disguise, but on the whole makes as humorless a partner as Thomaso does. Mrs. Behn, taking the dichotomy in his character literally, divides him into the gay Willmore and the more serious and moralistic Belvile.[12] Serulina becomes Florinda, and the two serious lovers are matched. For Willmore, she creates Hellena; their witty comedy of manners dialogues have no counterpart in *Thomaso.*

Killigrew's Edwardo and Ferdinando are Mrs. Behn's Blunt and Frederick. Lucetta and Sancho also have the same roles in both plays. This sub-plot in *The Rover* is developed in brief parts of two scenes in Acts I and II, in III.ii, in IV.iv, and in part of V.i. In *Thomaso* it takes up one full scene and parts of two others in the first two acts, two scenes in Act III, two in Act IV, at least six in Act V, and is continued in several scenes in Part Two. The proper subordination and economical management of this plot furnish a fine example of Mrs. Behn's craftsmanship.

Angelica is taken over with few changes except that in *Thomaso* she ends up happily on her way to Italy with the remaining unattached characters. Mrs. Behn cuts Saretta and Paulina, the other two courtesans; and with them goes a bulky and extremely dull plot which Killigrew cultivates extensively in Part Two. Throughout, the action itself is so rearranged that point by point comparison is difficult. The Willmore/

Belvile—Florinda episodes come from both parts of *Thomaso,* but mostly from Acts II and III of Part Two.[13] Blunt's gulling comes from the last half of Part One,[14] while the Angelica-Antonio-Pedro-Willmore plot comes from the first half of Part One and the last half·of Part Two.

The Second Part is adapted with even greater freedom. Beaumond is Killigrew's Harrigo, who appears frequently in both parts yet has no important plot function in either. Mrs. Behn adds Ariadne (and Lucia) to remedy this defect, taking hints from Serulina and Calis. Carlo combines Don Carlos and Don John in *Thomaso;* Blunt and Fetherfool are Edwardo and Ferdinando again; La Nuche is another Angelica. Shift and Hunt are additions. The farcical episodes with the giantess and dwarf are also additions since Killigrew never actually brings them on stage. Mrs. Behn's lapse in taste here is made up for at another point, however: for Killigrew's farce involving Lopus the mountebank and his magical baths, she substitutes the brilliant stratagem of having Willmore take Lopus' role. Much of the action in the last half of the play is original, especially in the main plot.

In both plays Mrs. Behn makes good use of Killigrew's language. Sometimes she follows an entire scene rather closely: Act II scene i of *The Rover,* for example, imitates Part One, Act II, scenes iii and iv. More often she uses several lines from *Thomaso* in an otherwise original speech, as in IV.ii or V.i. She obviously realized that Killigrew could write as well as or better than she; the number of his lines she used is proof sufficient, since her normal practice was to rewrite. Yet nowhere does she imitate his prolixity. Thomaso's first speeches to Angelica (I.ii.4) and Serulina (II.iii.3) are really astonishing: the latter contains over three hundred words. Lopus' initial address to the crowd (I.iv.2) furnishes another good example of her skill. In *Thomaso* it extends to two and a half folio pages; Mrs. Behn cuts it down and divides it into three parts with action between each. She borrows a few lines, but much of the patter and all of the satire are her own.

An adaptor could hardly do more than Mrs. Behn did with Killigrew's play. She found it a promising but interminable comedy which could not possibly be staged. Out of it she made two successful plays, one of them good enough to hold the boards for several decades. She focused and tightened a diffuse plot, made witty dialogue out of long speeches, replaced most of *Thomaso's* bawdy with genuine humor, and in Hellena created one of her finest characters.[15]

The last of her adaptations was *The Roundheads,* based on *The Rump; or, The Mirror of the Late Times* (1660) by John Tatham. Tatham's play is a wretched satire on the last days of the Commonwealth. Such structure as it has is given by its ridiculous version of history: Bertlam and Woodfleet dispute the crown, Lady Bertlam sets up for queen and lords it over Mrs. Cromwell, the populace revolts and humbles all of them on the eve of the Restoration. The play is almost wholly political; the romance between Bertlam's secretary Walker and Lady Bertlam's maid Priscilla is confined to these minor characters and to a few scenes.

Mrs. Behn preserves most of the action, but cuts the play by about half, especially the many scenes involving the soldiers and prentices. She preserves its essential crudity, even to many details of language. In fact, she adds a farcical scene in which the Committee of Safety get drunk and start a pillow dance. She omits Walker entirely, and thus his romance; she also drops the Frenchman who appears among the crowd in Act V, and the long scene in which Lady Bertlam interviews the astrologer Lilly (IV.i). Some transposition of scenes is made, notably of that involving the three lady petitioners (V.ii to II.i). Her structural revision is thorough and excellent.

To replace the excised material, Mrs. Behn creates two Cavaliers, Loveless and Freeman, and involves them in an intrigue with Lady Lambert and Lady Desbro. This intrigue becomes the main plot. She also adds Ananias Gogle, that fine satire on Puritan hypocrisy, and involves him in the intrigue. Her additions, though better than anything in *The Rump,* sharply contrast with the political farce, and *The Roundheads* must be regarded as a failure.

Of the seventeen plays unquestionably by Mrs. Behn, then, two are fully her own; three are slightly indebted to specific sources; seven borrow more or less extensively from earlier works; and five are adaptations. As the discussion has shown, Mrs. Behn found material in contemporary history, in French heroic romance, in Italian *commedia,* and in popular fiction.

Most of her borrowing, however, is from the drama of the seventeenth century, both English and French. She preferred the generation of Shirley, Middleton, and Massinger to that of Shakespeare and Jonson. But she also borrows from Richard Brome and Thomas Killigrew, dramatists who were more nearly her contemporaries. Her use of Molière is also contemporary, and typically English: she uses incidents and ideas for very different comic purposes.

Mrs. Behn normally relies on her sources for plot suggestions and character outline rather than for dialogue. If she borrows a plot, or part of one, she commonly alters it and makes it but one strand in her own action. In several plays, notably *Sir Patient Fancy, The Young King, The False Count,* and *The City Heiress,* plot strands are borrowed from different sources and fused into a whole. The result is the complicated intrigue of which Restoration audiences were so fond.

Whatever her source, she makes it her own. Close examination of her plays and their sources reveals her craftsmanship and her essential creativity. The adaptations are an excellent example: in every case they are better than their originals. It is interesting to note that all of them fall between 1676 and 1682, accounting for half her dramatic work in the period.[16] After *The Roundheads,* she did no more; perhaps its failure disillusioned her.

One must conclude with Langbaine that Mrs. Behn borrowed extensively, not because she lacked invention, but because she lacked money. Poetry did not pay at all; plays offered her a living, but only if one wrote them at a pace that any modern dramatist would consider intolerable. Dryden, with far more genius and a less desperate need for money, borrowed at least as much, and did not always leave it marble. Yet financial pressure was probably not her only motive. She seems to have been as interested in what could be done with material as in its origin. Such had been a normal attitude in the Renaissance, and such was still a common attitude in her day.

CHAPTER 6

The Poet

MOST of Mrs. Behn's poetry is occasional—the work of a professional dramatist with a considerable lyric talent and a constant need for money. For her plays she wrote prologues and epilogues, only occasionally obtaining them from a fellow writer; these works constitute a clearly defined group. A second grouping is more miscellaneous: some forty songs written to be sung within the plays, several sets of commendatory verses, a number of topical pieces, and several translations. Elegies and panegyrics, often written in the loosely organized irregular stanza popularized by Abraham Cowley a generation earlier, make up a final group. A brief study of some of these poems suggests Mrs. Behn's unusual versatility and shows the quality of her best work.

I *Prologues and Epilogues*

The prologues and epilogues are typical of the period. They are always in couplets, though mcre triplets appear than Pope would have approved; and they are usually satiric and topical. The speaker, usually one of the important characters in the piece, addresses the audience directly; comments on the state of the theater and of the playgoers are staple fare. The audience is rarely praised for its good taste; in one prologue after another Mrs. Behn criticizes the trend toward farce and "entertainment" which she saw debasing the legitimate stage:

> Alas! a poet's good for nothing now,
> Unless he have the knack of conjuring too;
> For 'tis beyond all natural sense to guess
> How their strange miracles are brought to pass.

> Your Presto Jack be gone, and come again,
> With all the hocus art of legerdemain;
> Your dancing tester, nutmeg, and your cups,
> Outdoes your heroes and your amorous fops.[1]

Some of the pieces document the change. The prologue to *The Emperor of the Moon*, for example, traces the progress of recent drama from heroic tragedy through "humbler comedy" to farce. The attack on the taste of the playgoer is conventional, of course, but it is made too often to have no basis in fact. The fore- and afterpieces themselves give at least two reasons for the decline in quality. One is the thinning audience, a basic economic fact which forced most playwrights to take any measures necessary to fill the house. The epilogue to *The Second Part of the Rover* speaks of the poets as kings of wit summoning their parliaments by playbill; the new play used to be "the speech that begs supply":

> But now—
> The scanted tribute is so slowly paid,
> Our poets must find out another trade;
> They've tried all ways th' insatiate clan to please;
> Have parted with their old prerogatives—
> Their birthright satiring, and their just pretense
> Of judging, even their own wit and sense—
> And write against their consciences, to show
> How dull they can be to comply with you.
> They've flattered all the mutineers i' th' nation,
> Grosser than e'er was done in dedication;
> Pleased your sick palates with fantastic wit,
> Such as was ne'er a treat before to th' pit;
> Giants, fat cardinals, Pope Joans, and friars,
> To entertain right worshipfuls and squires. . . .

The prologue to *Abdelazer* chides the gallants for having been so long absent and for coming "only on the first and second days"; the epilogue to *The Emperor of the Moon* laments that "Not one is left will write for thin third day."

The other reason suggested for the decline is the turbulent political situation. The actress Elizabeth Currer comes on stage at the start of *The Feigned Courtesans* to ask:

> Who would have thought such hellish times to've seen,
> When I should be neglected at eighteen?
> That youth and beauty should be quite undone,
> A pox upon the Whore of Babylon.

Apparently, many of the audience no longer supported the Tory side, particularly in the late 1670's and early 1680's: "And yet you'll come but once, unless by stealth, / Except the author be for commonwealth."[2]

The gallants and fops who made up a large share of the audience are often baited in a good-humored way, especially for their capriciousness and love for the cheap and spectacular: "Vain amorous coxcombs every where are found, / Fops for all uses but the stage abound."[3] The prologue to *The Young King*, in like vein, mocks the "Sparks who are of noise and nonsense full, / At fifteen witty, and at twenty dull." But a stronger lash is reserved for country squires, city merchants, and of course Puritans. The country bumpkin "At last by happy chance is hither led, / To purchase clap with loss of maidenhead"; he comes to be "all burlesque in mode and dress," and nothing more than "mighty noise and show."[4] The "cit" is often an upstart, and nearly always Whiggish. Satire against the Whigs is both general and specific, as in the references to the *Ignoramus* jury and to Titus Oates. Mrs. Behn follows the Tory line in identifying Shaftesbury and his group with the cant and violence of the Good Old Cause. The prologue to *The Roundheads*, a typical example, has the ghost of Hewson "Roused by strange scandal from th' eternal flame" to ask whether all the furor over Jesuit plots can "Act mischief equal to Presbytery":

> Pay those that rail, and those that can delude
> With scribbling nonsense the loose multitude.
> Pay well your witnesses, they may not run
> To the right side, and tell who set 'em on.
> Pay 'em so well, that they may ne'er recant,
> And so turn honest merely out of want.
> Pay juries, that no formal laws may harm us;
> Let treason be secured by *Ignoramus*.

The political theme appears in some form in nearly half of the twenty-two prologues and epilogues presumably written by

Mrs. Behn. The epilogue to *The Rover* draws an analogy between Puritanism and those who would "with canting rule . . . the stage refine," and Mrs. Behn attacks "dull method" also in the prologue to *The Amorous Prince* and in the epilogue to *Sir Patient Fancy.* The reverse of the coin appears in the frequent panegyrics to Charles and his policies. The epilogue to *The Young King,* for example, develops a not so obscure contrast between the Arcadian shepherd in peaceful command of his flock and the chaotic state of England; the concluding reference, "And keep the golden age within our woods and plains," makes use of an image common in Tory poetry.

Many, if not all, of these themes appear frequently in prologues and epilogues by other hands; they occasionally serve to confirm and emphasize themes in the plays they accompany, but only more personal themes like the defense of women in the epilogue to *Sir Patient Fancy* and in the prologue to *The Forced Marriage* are peculiar to Mrs. Behn.

Mrs. Behn's handling of the couplet form is usually competent and often distinguished. Sustained metaphors like that in the epilogue to Part Two of *The Rover* (above, p. 103) remind one of Dryden, the greatest master of the genre. The form demands an ear for the rhythms of speech, and the technical skill to achieve variety and interest within the limitations of the two-line unit. Mrs. Behn has both. In one piece after another she manages to bring off a good-humored attack on the foibles of her audience, allude satirically to contemporary politics, and simultaneously evoke the mood most suitable for introducing her play and for bringing the evening to a close. The prologue to *Sir Patient Fancy,* spoken by the actor Thomas Betterton, adopts the bantering, familiar tone characteristic of the period:

> Oh the great blessing of a little wit!
> I've seen an elevated poet sit
> And hear the audience laugh and clap, yet say,
> Gad, after all, 'tis a damned silly play;
> He, unconcerned, cries only—Is it so?
> No matter, these unwitty things will do
> When your fine, fustian, useless eloquence
> Serves but to chime asleep a drowsy audience.
> Who at the vast expense of wit would treat,
> That might so cheaply please the appetite?

The positioning of *great* and *little,* the irony of *blessing,* and the pun of *elevated* are important details. The rhymes in lines 2, 3, and 4 are naturally produced without inversion of normal syntax; the use of the pyrrhic foot in line 3, forcing a slight accent on the *yet,* emphasizes the disjunction stated in the couplet and the variability of the audience. Mrs. Behn places her caesuras to achieve maximum variety within the lines, and she guards against monotony by varying iambs with trochees (ll. 1 and 9) and by using polysyllables in almost every line. The alexandrine in line 8 is perhaps too obviously the metrical equivalent of *drowsy,* but the alliteration and accent shift in *fine fustian* produce exactly the desired effect.

Mrs. Behn rarely uses the superb organizing images which inform Dryden's best prologues. But the political situation provides her with a ready-made metaphor which she manipulates with great skill. The same prologue furnishes a good example:

> But now, like happy states luxurious grown,
> The monarch wit unjustly you dethrone,
> And a tyrannic commonwealth prefer,
> Where each small wit starts up and claims his share;
> And all those laurels are in pieces torn,
> Which did e'er while one sacred head adorn.

The *sacred head* is Dryden, but the metaphor takes the passage beyond a single literary figure. Dryden becomes Charles; his "dethronement" by a mob of hack poets and pamphleteers is made to suggest not merely the destruction of literary values but the fate of the royal martyr and its consequences in the Commonwealth period. The use of the word *sacred* establishes still another level of meaning: beyond the "death" of Dryden is the death of Charles; beyond it is that of Christ. The effect of the passage is to connect two apparently unrelated phenomena—the state of literature and the state of the nation; assert that the one is caused by the other; and use the religious image to condemn republicanism in all three areas of life.

A final example of her skill may be cited from the prologue to *The City Heiress,* which uses an extended metaphor from the business world to satirize an abortive dinner of "thanksgiving" planned by the Whigs to discomfit the Tories:

> Who, but the most incorrigible fops,
> For ever doomed in dismal cells, called shops,
> To cheat and damn themselves to get their livings,
> Would lay sweet money out in sham Thanksgivings?
> Sham-plots, you may have paid for o'er and o'er;
> But whoe'er paid for a sham treat before?
> Had you not better sent your offerings all
> Hither to us, than Sequestrators Hall?
> I being your steward, justice had been done ye;
> I could have entertained you worth your money.

In ten lines, Mrs. Behn identifies the leading Whigs as foppish shopkeepers, refers slyly to the collapse of the Oates plot, and wittily suggests that her Tory play would have been better entertainment for the Whigs than anything they themselves could have planned for the same money.

II   *Songs and Other Short Poems*

The Restoration wits perfected a sophisticated and impersonal style which for elegance, wit, and precision of tone has seldom been surpassed in English poetry. The mode they adopted was limited and artificial, but its limits were self-imposed and its artificiality deliberate. Mrs. Behn's best songs bear comparison with those of the court poets and of Matthew Prior; few of them fail to give pleasure after nearly three hundred years.

Her lyric gift is evident from the first. The masque in Act V of *The Forced Marriage* is graceful enough, but the page's song in II.vi is at another level of achievement:

> Amintas that true-hearted swain
> Upon a river's bank was laid,
> Where to the pitying streams he did complain
> On Sylvia that false charming maid;
> But she was still regardless of his pain.
> Oh! faithless Sylvia! would he cry,
> And what he said the echoes would reply:
>   Be kind or else I die. E[cho]. I die.
>   Be kind or else I die. E[cho]. I die.

The sophisticated pastoralism exemplified by the conscious and half-ironic use of personification *(pitying streams)* and by the

light oxymoron (false charming) is quite typical. Mrs. Behn
accepts both the language and the themes dictated by the convention; the names and the setting are as appropriate as the
sentiments. The stylization is obvious, the lyric quality and
the handling of rhythm exceptional.

Other fine examples are Hippolita's song in III.iii of *The
Dutch Lover* (cited in Chapter Two), and the song for II.vi of
the same play:

> His charming eyes no aid required,
> To tell their amorous tale:
> On her that was already fired
> 'Twas easy to prevail.
> He did but kiss, and clasp me round,
> Whilst they his thoughts expressed;
> And gently laid me on the ground—
> Ah! Who can guess the rest?

The later plays show no decline in Mrs. Behn's powers.
The magnificent song which opens *Abdelazer*—"Love in Fantastic Triumph Sat"—has been often reprinted, and is probably
her best known poem.[5] The songs in *The Town Fop* are almost
as good. The comic serenade in *Sir Patient Fancy* (III.ix) is
deliberately bathetic and beautifully illuminates Sir Credulous'
character. Both *The Second Part of the Rover* and *The City
Heiress* contain fine songs: Sir Anthony's catch in Act III scene
i of the latter is as appropriate for him as for the situation in
which it occurs.

All of these songs come early in Mrs. Behn's career. Many of
them were collected in her *Poems upon Several Occasions:
With a Voyage to the Island of Love* (1684).[6] By that time she
had written a considerable number of other lyrics. Some of
them, like "Our Cabal," have unclear biographical significance;
most are in the usual pastoral vein, as artless as art could make
them, and written with that detached gaiety so typical of the
Restoration period and so foreign to the twentieth century. The
last stanza of "When Jemmy First Began to Love" is a good
example:

> But now for Jemmy must I mourn,
> Who to the wars must go;
> His sheephook to a sword must turn:
> Alack, what shall I do?

> His bagpipe into warlike sounds,
> Must now exchanged be:
> Instead of bracelets, fearful wounds;
> Then what becomes of me? (p. 50)

Additional lyrics appeared in *Miscellany, Being A Collection of Poems by Several Hands* (1685), a volume edited by Mrs. Behn. Among them is the worst of her poems, a painful paraphrase of the Lord's Prayer, but also the excellent song, "Cease, Cease, Aminta to Complain," and a graceful dialogue "made in an entertainment at court." The last substantial group of poems is found in *A Miscellany of New Poems*, appended to *Lycidus; or, The Lover in Fashion* (1688). No songs are among them, and such poems as the two to Alexis add nothing to her earlier achievements. By this time she was near death, and much involved in fiction and translation—activities that seem to have brought in more money than lyric poetry. After her death, poems by her, or attributed to her, appeared for a number of years; but none of them matches the quality of the dozen or so songs already mentioned.

Among Mrs. Behn's shorter poems are a number of narrative and satiric efforts, and a few miscellaneous pieces. The narratives are distinctly inferior to the lyrics, partly because Mrs. Behn's handling of rhythm and rhyme in them is inadequate. "On a Juniper Tree," for example, is written in tetrameter couplets and seems to end every few lines. The reader comes down hard on the rhymes; only one line in six or seven has any internal pause. "Our Cabal," written in the same form, is not much better. The only good narrative poem is a paraphrase of an unnamed French original, entitled "The Disappointment." She adopts a more flexible rhyme scheme to tell Lysander's story in stanzas, and the effect is that of a series of short lyrics held together by the sequence of action.

Satiric poems are rare outside the prologues and epilogues. "A Letter to a Brother of the Pen in Tribulation" is one example; the best is her verses "On a Conventicle," first printed in Charles Gildon's *Miscellany Poems upon Several Occasions* (1692):

> Behold that race, whence England's woes proceed,
> The viper's nest, where all our mischiefs breed,
> There, guided by inspiration, treason speaks,
> And through the holy bagpipe Legion squeaks.

The Nation's curse, religion's ridicule,
The rabble's God, the politician's tool,
Scorn of the wise, and scandal of the just,
The villain's refuge, and the women's lust.

III *Elegies and Panegyrics*

The last group of Mrs. Behn's original poems—the elegies and
panegyrics—bulks larger than all the rest. The poems comprising it are occasional in the strict sense of that word: they are
written upon someone's birth, death, or marriage; upon a friend's
departure; or perhaps upon a fellow author's new book. Most
of them are addressed to members of the royal family or to the
nobility and are at least semi-public in character. These circumstances dictated an elevated form. Mrs. Behn ordinarily
chose the pindaric, the highest suitable form in the contemporary hierarchy of genres; less frequently, she used the couplet.

Some poems in this type appeared in the early collections.
The 1684 *Poems* contains "The Golden Age"; "A Farewell to
Celadon, on His Going into Ireland"; "On the Death of Mr.
Grinhil, the Famous Painter"; "To Mr. Creech . . . on His Excellent Translation of Lucretius"; "To Mrs. W. On Her Excellent Verses . . ."; "To My Lady Morland at Tunbridge"; "On
Mr. J. H. in a Fit of Sickness"; and "To the Honorable Edward
Howard. . . ." Of these, only the poem to Lady Morland is in
regular couplet form; most are irregular in both rhyme scheme
and meter. Most of them are conventional and overly rhetorical; they tell the reader very little about their subjects and
sound, therefore, like a hundred other forgotten pieces written
on similar occasions.

One, however, is of greater interest. The poem on the golden
age, which opens the volume, is a free paraphrase of an English
translation from the French. Its pastoral primitivism recalls
Mrs. Behn's earliest plays, and adumbrates more than one passage in *Oronooko*. The versification is undistinguished; in fact,
part of the first stanza is cited in *Peri Bathous* as an example of
the florid style.[7] But the poem is the author's most explicit
statement of a major theme: the conflict between sex and society. In the Edenic world of the poem, in which "Right and

Property were words since made" (p. 5), lovers are restrained only by their vows to each other, which are "inviolably true":

> Not kept in fear of gods, no fond religious cause,
> Nor in obedience to the duller laws.
> Those fopperies of the gown were then not known,
> Those vain, those politic curbs to keep man in,
> Who by a fond mistake created that a sin
> Which freeborn we, by right of nature, claim own own.
>
> (p. 8)

Honor is society's invention, designed to destroy paradise:

> Honor! that put'st our words that should be free
> Into a set formality;
> Thou base debaucher of the generous heart,
> That teachest all our looks and actions art;
> What love designed a sacred gift,
> What nature made to be possessed,
> Mistaken honor, made a theft. . . .   (p. 10)

Honor belongs to courts and palaces, where it may disturb the politician's sleep. The natural man, aware that beyond death is an eternal night, seizes his chance for happiness: "The swift paced hours of life soon steal away: / Stint not, ye Gods, his short-lived joy" (p. 11).

The *Miscellany* of 1685 added four more poems to this group: "On the Death of the Late Earl of Rochester"; "A Pindaric to Mr. P. Who Sings Finely"; "On the Author of . . . *The Way to Health . . .*"; and "A Pastoral to Mr. Stafford . . ." None of these is especially good, but the poem to Rochester is remarkable for genuineness of feeling. Mrs. Behn admired him both as man and as poet: "He was but lent this duller world t' improve / In all the charms of poetry, and love" (p. 45). Finally, the poems at the end of *Lycidus* included "On the Honourable Sir Francis Fane . . .", "A Pastoral Pindaric . . . ," and "On Desire." The second of these states again the superiority of love to the restrictions of society. Dorset and his wife will be happy because their marriage was not determined by "portion and jointure" but by common interest and affection.

[111]

Many poems in the form, and particularly those written on state occasions, were published in folio or quarto shortly after the event which they celebrate. The first of these was *A Pindaric on the Death of Our Late Sovereign* (early 1685), which had a second London and a Dublin edition within the year. Mrs. Behn's Tory sentiments are nowhere more obvious than in this elegy, which compares Charles with both Christ and Moses and which draws the logical conclusion about Charles' ultimate destiny: like Christ, he fell "a bleeding victim to atone for all!" and, "transfigured all to glory, mounts to Heaven!" (st. 4). *A Poem Humbly Dedicated to the Great Pattern of Piety and Virtue Catherine Queen Dowager*, published later in 1685, indulges in hyperboles on her grief and carries on the metaphor of divine correspondence: "So the blest Virgin at the world's great loss, / Came, and beheld, then fainted at the cross."[8]

The last, and by far the longest, of the 1685 poems is *A Pindaric Poem on the Happy Coronation of . . . James II.* Mrs. Behn's joy in the event is unfeigned; the Gods themselves are happy in her poem:

> Gay robes of light the young divinities put on,
> And spread their shining locks to outvie the sun.
> On pillows formed of yielding air they lie,
> Placed in the mid-way regions of the sky. . . .   (st. 4)

The elaborate description of the coronation is not very good. The verse is frequently stilted and artificial, the flattery gross if not fulsome, and the sentiments expressed in exaggerated diction. Occasionally the poem, like that on the death of Charles, comes alive, especially when Mrs. Behn deals with her personal feeling about the Stuarts:

> Howe'er I toil for life all day,
> With whate'er cares my soul's oppressed,
> 'Tis in that sunshine still I play,
> 'Tis there my wearied mind's at rest;
> But oh vicisitudes of night must come
> Between the rising glories of the sun!   (st. 19)

When the personal note is missing, these poems become mere hack work, praise tailored in advance of an order and perhaps never paid for. The pindaric *To . . . Christopher Duke of Albemarle* (1687) is perhaps the worst of the entire group, largely for this reason. On the other hand, the elegy *To the Memory of . . . George Duke of Buckingham,* published in May, 1687,[9] is surprisingly good. Mrs. Behn, who obviously regarded this celebrated wit very highly, rises to her occasion. "When so much wit, wit's great reformer dies," the very muses come to his obsequies. Care may dog the steps of the ordinary statesman, but in his handling of the ship of state,

> Great Buckingham a sprightlier measure trod:
> When o're the mounting waves the vessel rod[e],
> Unshocked by toils, by tempests undismayed,
> Steered the great bark, and as that danced, he played.
>
> (ll. 39-42)

He was a phoenix, but with a difference:

> Thy matchless worth all successors defies,
> And scorned an heir should from thy ashes rise:
> Begins and finishes that glorious sphere
> Too mighty for a second charioteer. (ll. 80-83)

During her last days, Mrs. Behn published panegyrics on every important Tory occasion, probably because her financial need was great. The Queen's pregnancy produced the appropriate congratulation, full of Tory imagery:

> Like the first sacred infant, this will come
> With promise laden from the blessed womb,
> To call the wand'ring scattered nations home.
> Adoring princes shall arrive from far,
> Informed by angels, guided by his star,
> The new-born wonder to behold, and greet;
> And kings shall offer incense at his feet.[10]

The subsequent poem on the birth of the Prince of Wales,[11] in its delight at the perpetuation of the Stuart line, is more than a

little ironic in its references to the future of the prince who became the Pretender: "No monarch's birth was ever ushered
in / With signs so fortunate as this has been" (st. 3). Sir Roger
L'Estrange's *History of the Times* occasioned a poem to this
loyal Tory (1688), but the events of that memorable year were
fatal to Mrs. Behn's political hopes, and the two subsequent
panegyrics are markedly different in tone.

*A Congratulatory Poem to . . . Queen Mary upon Her Arrival
in England*[12] presents its author bewailing "an unhappy dear
loved monarch's fate"; her stubborn muse lay "sullen with stubborn loyalty," aroused only by the memory of Mary's blood relationship to Charles II:

> And thou, great lord of all my vows, permit
> My muse who never failed obedience yet,
> To pay her tribute at Maria's feet,
> Maria so divine a part of you,
> Let me be just—but just with honor too.
>
> (ll. 54-58)

The last of these poems was written during Mrs. Behn's fatal
illness. Gilbert Burnet, the great Whig divine, had considerately
inquired about her health, and the pindaric to him was her re-
sponse. His writings, she says, have almost persuaded her of the
justice of the Glorious Revolution. But old loyalties are stronger,
and in the fourth and sixth stanzas of the poem she presents her
case in the most moving lines in all her poetry:

> My muse that would endeavor fain to glide
> With the fair prosperous gale, and the full driving tide:
> But loyalty commands with pious force,
> That stops me in the thriving course;
> The breeze that wafts the crowding nations o'er,
> Leaves me unpitied far behind
> On the forsaken, barren shore,
> To sigh with Echo, and the murmuring wind. . . .
> Thus while the chosen seed possess the promised land,
> I, like the excluded prophet, stand;
> The fruitful happy soil can only see,
> But am forbid by fate's decree
> To share the triumph of the joyful victory.

[114]

> Though I the wond'rous change deplore,
> That makes me useless and forlorn,
> Yet I the great design adore,
> Though ruined in the universal turn.
> Nor can my indigence and lost repose,
> Those meager furies that surround me close,
>   Convert my sense and reason more
>   To this unprecedented enterprise,
>   Than that a man so great, so learn'd, so wise,
> The brave achievement owns and nobly justifies.   (sts. 6, 8)

Few Whigs had so generous and sincere a compliment from an ardent Tory, and few monarchs can have had such unswerving loyalty where there was no obligation and very little reward. One must pity the blindness of Mrs. Behn's devotion, especially in the case of James II; but one cannot help admiring its integrity and strength.

The substantial poems Mrs. Behn produced for great occasions have been largely forgotten and do not merit revival. The handful of exquisite lyrics, slight as they are, have proved less ephemeral: it is owing to them and to her prologues and epilogues that she may claim a place as a minor Restoration poet.

CHAPTER 7

The Translator

SOONER or later Aphra Behn tried her hand at almost every literary activity, and she managed to produce something of worth in all of them. Translating came fairly late in her career; this fact and the miscellaneous titles suggest that she engaged in this kind of work more for money than love. Yet it is clear that by the middle 1680's, at least, her abilities were well enough recognized by her contemporaries. If she began as a publisher's hack, she improved this status before many years had passed.

I Ovid's Epistles

Dryden (or the publisher Jacob Tonson) gave her a start by accepting "A Paraphrase on Oenone to Paris" for inclusion in *Ovid's Epistles, Translated by Several Hands* (1680). "I was desired to say," he writes in his preface, "that the author, who is of the fair sex, understood not Latin. But if she does not, I am afraid she has given us occasion to be ashamed who do."[1] Mrs. Behn's version is, as one would expect, a loose paraphrase; Dryden, whose famous definitions of metaphrase, paraphrase, and imitation grace the same preface, remarks that it "is in Mr. Cowley's way of imitation only." The story of the nymph's complaint to Paris is followed fairly closely, but the thinness of the plot allows for considerable interpolation, which Mrs. Behn makes full use of. The following passage, in which only the first eight lines follow Ovid, is representative:

> A spotless maid into thy arms I brought,
> Untouched in fame, even innocent in thought;
> Whilst she with love has treated many a guest,
> And brings thee but the leavings of a feast:
> With Theseus from her country made escape,

Whilst she miscalled the willing flight, a rape.
So now from Atreus' son, with thee is fled,
And still the rape hides the adult'rous deed.
And is it thus great ladies keep entire
That virtue they so boast, and you admire?
Is this a trick of courts? Can ravishment
Serve for a poor evasion of consent?
Hard shift to save that honor prized so high,
Whilst the mean fraud's the greater infamy.
How much more happy are we rural maids,
Who know no other palaces than shades;
Who want no titles to enslave the crowd,
Lest they should babble all our crimes aloud;
No arts our good to show, our ills to hide,
Nor know to cover faults of love with pride.
I loved, and all love's dictates did pursue,
And never thought it could be sin with you.
To gods and men I did my love proclaim;
For one soft hour with thee, my charming swain,
Would recompence an age to come of shame,
Could it as well but satisfy my fame.
But oh! Those tender hours are fled and lost,
And I no more of fame, or thee, can boast!
'Twas thou wert honor, glory, all, to me:
Till swains had learned the vice of perjury,
No yielding maids were charged with infamy.
'Tis false and broken vows make love a sin,
Hadst thou been true, we innocent had been.[2]

The mocking reference to the honor of "great ladies," the pastoralism of the lines about "rural maids," and especially the idea that love is sinful only if the lovers are false to their own agreement are themes quite characteristic of the translator. In technique, the lines are undistinguished: Mrs. Behn uses internal pause in a third of them, yet they lack rhythmic variety. The words flow readily, but the result is pedestrian. The possibilities for antithesis and balance are rarely exploited, and the lines are more distinguished for the naturalness of the rhymes than for their tropes or figures. The translation is not unworthy of the volume, but it is one to which the modern reader is unlikely to return. Mrs. Behn ended her 1684 *Poems* with the piece, slightly revised, and the original volume went through several editions. Both facts suggest that her contemporaries did not too greatly mind her small Latin and less Greek.

II The Voyage to the Island of Love

Her second effort is more interesting. To the *Poems* of 1684 she appended a translation of the Abbé Paul Tallemant's sentimental fantasy *Le voyage de l'isle d'amour*, a work originally published at Paris in 1663. Tallemant's elegant little piece runs to some forty pages and is in prose interspersed with songs. Mrs. Behn puts the narrative part into couplets and sets off the songs by the use of various stanzaic patterns. She follows the meager plot of the original quite closely, maintaining the sequence of personified abstractions which confront Lysander in his lover's progress toward Aminta—Respect, Inquietude, Hope, the City of Discretion, the Den of Cruelty, the River of Despair, the Bower of Bliss. But she expands the whole work by at least a third, and the poems in the English version do not always correspond with those in the French.

It is difficult now to recapture the mood required to appreciate *The Voyage*. It is delicate, sophisticated, trivial yet not at all banal—the product of the same aristocratic leisure which produced the *romans de la longue haleine* and the bluestocking salons. Mrs. Behn's translation, or rather adaptation, is very well done. The choice of couplets for Tallemant's prose is curious; since she reverted to prose for the sequel, one must assume she did not care to repeat the experiment. But in this case her couplets, used largely for narrative purposes and set down with a lightness and lack of pretension suitable to the subject, are often successful. Lysander thus describes the voyage to the "far country called Content":

> The sails were hoisted, and the streamers spread,
> And cheerfully we cut the yielding flood;
> Calm was the sea, and peaceful every wind,
> As if the gods had with our wishes joined
> To make us prosperous; all the whispering air
> Like lovers' joys, was soft, and falsely fair.   (p. 5)

The sensuousness of the translation is greater than that of the original, and so is the amount of detail:

[118]

> The cowslip, lily, rose and jesamine,
> The daffodil, the pink and eglantine,
> Whose gawdy store continues all the year,
> Makes but the meanest of the wonders here. (p. 11)

The passage is particularly English, as is the satire which creeps into the first description of the island's inhabitants:

> There an old battered fop you might behold
> Lavish his love, discretion, and his gold
> On a fair she, that has a trick in art,
> To cheat him of his politics and heart;
> Whilst he that jilts the nation o'er and o'er,
> Wants sense to find it in the subtler w---re. (p. 12)

The lyrics of *The Voyage* are similar to the couplets in tone, though loosely set off from the narrative by such titles as "Love's Power," "The Reflection," "Absence," and "The Loss." The stanzaic patterns vary, but many use the simple ballad quatrain, with lines of different length. They are best when songlike; it is no wonder Blake and Swinburne admired her lyric gifts:

> The virgin here shows no disdain,
> Nor does the shepherd sigh in vain:
> This knows no cruelty, nor that no pain. . . . (p. 119)

One gets a good idea of Mrs. Behn's treatment of her original by comparing the two accounts of Lysander's reaction to Aminta's death. Tallemant is concise and matter of fact:

Au milieu de mes délices, un matin je vis un homme qui effrontément vint troubler mes plaisirs. Il avoit l'air majestueux & indépendant. La physionomie haute, & les yeux & le front d'un homme absolu, & qui ne fait ce que c'est que d'obéir. En un mot, c'étoit le destin, dont les arrêts sont irrévocables, qui enleva Amynte d'entre mes bras. Tous mes efforts ne purent l'empêcher, & il l'emmena je ne sais où car je n'en ai pu avoir de nouvelles depuis ce tems là: je quittai aussi tôt le palais du vrai plaisir, qui me sembloit désagréable, puisqu' Amynte n'y étoit plus, & je me vins retirer en ce lieu, où je crois passer le reste des jours qu m'accordera ma douleur.[3]

The translator expands this to sixty-three lines. She laments the evil day and the shortness of human life, adds a tender fare-well speech by Aminta, and details every aspect of Lysander's grief. The personification of destiny is dropped as too abstract; emotion replaces the laconic detachment of the original:

> The fading roses of her lips I press,
> But no kind word the silenced prattlers will confess;
> Her lovely eyes I kiss and call upon,
> But all their wonted answering rhetoric's gone.   (p. 126)

It is evident *The Voyage* and its sequel *Lycidus* are not mere hack translations but adaptations worthy, like *The Rover,* of in-dependent consideration.

III   Seneca Unmasked

That Mrs. Behn could go from Tallemant to La Rochefoucauld is evidence of her great versatility. Her translation, entitled *Seneca Unmasked; or, Moral Reflections,* was appended to the *Miscellany* of 1685 and comprised pages 301-82 of that work. She translates nearly four hundred of the maxims, and is gen-erally as concise and forceful here as she was graceful and discursive in *The Voyage.* Her diction and syntax are on the whole simple and straightforward, and one knows from the pref-ace that she deliberately avoided the formal sentences of some of her contemporaries. "I must own," she writes, "I always pre-fer that unstudied and undesigned way of writing (though not so approved of by the learned) which is used by a courtier who has wit, as that of the late Lord Rochester and present Lord Mulgrave, to the regularities tortured and wracked by many other stiff writers, whose judgment is better than their wit or natural fancy . . ." [XI^v].

Her translation of La Rochefoucauld, though not the first, is satisfactory throughout and often excellent. Its flavor is best shown by examples, chosen from among the most famous of the *Maxims:*

We have all strength enough to bear the misfortunes of others.

⁎   ⁎   ⁎

We promise according to our hopes, and perform according to our fears.

Everybody complains of his want of memory; but few, or none, of their want of judgment.

✿   ✿   ✿

Hypocrisy is the homage that vice pays to virtue.

✿   ✿   ✿

It is with love as with apparitions: all the world talks of 'em, but few have seen 'em.[4]

Mrs. Behn obviously realizes that interpolation is out of place and that the English must attempt, even if it cannot duplicate, the ironic tone and the great energy of the French.

IV   The Lover's Watch

From this task she turned again to the Arcadian writers. In 1686 appeared *La Montre; or, The Lover's Watch*, an adaptation of Balthasar de Bonnecorse's work of the same name. The French work, a kind of hothouse courtesy book, was published in two parts, the first containing *The Watch* (1666), the second *The Case* and *The Mirror* (1671). Mrs. Behn includes all three parts, preserving Bonnecorse's titles. The idea behind them is identical. In *The Watch* Iris has sent Damon "a watch of my fashion," divided into the twenty-four hours of the day. His duties, especially to their love, are prescribed and recounted in graceful prose interspersed with lyrics. Damon provides the watch with a case and describes to her its figure, four ciphers, and clasp. In the final section, he sends her a mirror, which eulogizes her shape, complexion, and other features—not to mention her discretion and goodness. These sections, like the first, are mixed prose and verse.

Mrs. Behn follows the same procedure she used for *The Voyage*, but keeps the text in prose. The original is expanded nearly twofold; for example, the "dinner hour" in Bonnecorse takes up some seventy words plus two four-line poems, but the translation expands the discussion to four hundred words and adds a twenty-four line poem. The English version adds titles for the poems, but otherwise follows the pattern of the original. Once or twice Mrs. Behn inserts quite new material: she adds to the patriotism of Bonnecorse (in "Divers Dreams") her own Royalist opinions and mentions names of those she approves of, like Buckingham. Her fluency in French is incontestable, yet the flavor she gives to the work is unmistakably English. Comparison shows the careless ease and the added detail characteristic of her style:

Les Yeux d'Iris

Ie ne sçay si vous ne serez point eblouyé de l'éclat de vos yeux, ills sont du plus beau bleu qu'on puisse voir, & leurs regards aussi doux que languissans, portent tousiours des coups inévitables.[5]

Iris's Eyes

I believe, my fair mistress, I shall dazzle you with the luster of your own eyes. They are the finest blue in the world: they have all the sweetness that ever charmed the heart; with a certain languishment, that's irresistible; and never any looked on 'em, that did not sigh after 'em. Believe me, Iris, they carry unavoidable darts and fires; and whoever expose themselves to their dangers, pay for their imprudence.

V Aesop's Fables

In 1687, Francis Barlow, a famous artist whose engravings of animals and birds were widely admired, published an elaborate folio edition of Aesop: *Aesop's Fables with His Life: in English, French and Latin.* He tells the reader that "the ingenious Mrs. A. Behn has been so obliging as to perform the English poetry, which in short comprehends the sense of the fable and moral; whereof to say much were needless, since it may sufficiently recommend itself to all persons of understanding."[6] She contributed thirty-two quatrains for the biographical plates, and one hundred and ten to the fables. To each of the latter group she added a couplet "moral." The translator must have enjoyed her task: the volume is a good example of contemporary book production, and her poems appeared just below the half-page engravings on the recto pages.

This work, mentioned briefly by Woodcock and hardly noticed elsewhere,[7] is quite interesting. The quatrains themselves are competent and often extremely good. In general, they follow the sense of the Latin and French versions and relate fairly directly to the illustration. But in nearly a quarter of the total, Mrs. Behn manages to introduce topical allusions to English society which fall into several categories. Some demonstrate

her loyalty to the Stuarts, that for the story of the lion and the
mouse, for example: "Do not despise the service of a slave, / An
oak did once a glorious monarch save" (Fable 23). When the
biography recounts the story of the monument erected by the
Delphians to get rid of the plague caused by their unjust murder
of the fabulist, Mrs. Behn does not miss the opportunity:

Thus did not our ungrateful British brood
To expiate for guiltless royal blood;
Had we thy sacred name, great Charles, immortal made,
We'd shunned those plagues the wiser Delphians stayed. (Plate 31)

Several other couplets refer to the ill-starred Duke of Monmouth. The story of the kite, frog, and mouse is glossed with
such a reference: "The fond aspiring youth who empire sought /
by dire ambition was to ruin brought" (Fable 35). Finally,
a few poems allude to the political situation in broader terms
and to other prominent persons. The tale of the lion and other
beasts is used to defend the Tory principle of the King's "whole
prerogative," that of the ass in lion's skin seems to hit at the
Earl of Shaftesbury, and one for the biography clearly attacks
Titus Oates.[8]

Not all the references are political. Some refer to the literary
scene, like Plate 28 in the biographical section. Aesop has his
monument, but "In this dull age, no statues are allowed, / But
Dryden too must fall i' th' undistinguished crowd." Others attack
the foibles of society: the fable of the ox and toad (Number 26)
is used to satirize the "would-be wits"; and that of the jay and
peacock is given a characteristic Restoration turn: "Tis the gay
dress that makes the lover dote, / Not the fine soul, but the
fine petticoat" (Number 47). And one or two reintroduce a
theme familiar to any reader of the plays: "Tis death to youth
by age to be embraced, / And winter's snow June's gay roses
blast" (Fable 61). The examples cited demonstrate once again
Mrs. Behn's freedom as a translator and adaptor, and the suita-
bility of the "imitation" technique to her artistic temperament.

VI *Translations from Fontenelle*

The next year, one of the most prolific in her career, saw the
publication of no less than four full-length adaptations. One—
Agnes de Castro—is a novel, and will be taken up in a later

chapter. Two are translations from B. Le Bovier de Fontenelle, and one is a continuation of the *Voyage to the Island of Love.*

The volume published in English as *The History of Oracles, and the Cheats of the Pagan Priests* (1688) goes back to an early semi-anthropological work by Antonious van Dale, published in Amsterdam in 1683 under the title *De oraculis ethnicorum dissertationes duae. . . .* Fontenelle translated the volume as *Histoire des oracles* (Paris, 1686); Mrs. Behn's version is a fairly close reading of the French—a translation of a translation. There is very little interpolation or expansion, as a comparison of the two passages below will indicate:

Aussi voit-on toute la religion payenne ne demandoit que des ceremonies, & nuls sentimens du coeur. Les dieux sont irritez, tous leurs foudres sont prests à tomber, comment les appaisera-t-on? Faut-il se répentir des crimes quon a commis? Faut-il rentrer dans les voyes de la justice naturelle qui devroit estre entre tous les hommes? Point du tout. Il faut seulement prendre un veau de telle couleur, né en tel temps, l'égorger avec un tel couteau, & cela desarmera tous les dieux. Encore vous est-il permis de vous moquer en vous-mesmes du sacrifice, si vous voulez, il n'en ira pas plus mal.   (pp. 96-97)

So that we may see all the pagan religion was mere ceremony, in which the mind bore no part. The Gods are angry, their thunder is ready to be discharged, how shall they be appeased? Must we repent us of the crimes we have committed? Must we re-enter into the paths of that natural justice which ought to be among all men? Not at all; we need only take a calf of such a color, calved at such a time, and cut the throat of it with such a knife, and this will disarm the wrath of all the Gods: Nay, farther, it is permitted you to laugh at the sacrifice, if you have a mind to it; 'twill go never the worse with you.   (pp. 64-65)

If anything, Mrs. Behn stays too close to French idiom in this work: her own style is more natural, and so is that of her other translations. Since her version is also rather literal, the reader's interest centers on van Dale and not on Aphra Behn.

This judgment seems also valid for *A Discovery of New Worlds* (1688), a translation of an original book by Fontenelle entitled *Entretiens sur la pluralité des mondes* (Paris, 1686). Her version was not the first in English, and the modern reader is likely to be as interested in "The Translator's Preface" as in

[124]

the body of the work. She began, she says, with the idea that "an Englishwoman might venture to translate any thing a Frenchwoman may be supposed to have spoken. But when I had made a trial, I found the task not so easy as I believed at first . . ." (Sig. A4). She agrees with the Earl of Roscommon that the nearer two languages agree in "idioms or turn of the phrase," the easier the translator's task becomes. Italian and Spanish, she feels, are closer to Latin than French and thus easier to translate. (Mrs. Behn shared the common but erroneous view that English was derived from Latin.) Among other reasons for the difficulty, she cites the differences between English and French temperament, the great changes in the French language in the previous hundred years, and the fondness of the French for "words they steal from other languages" ([A4ᵛ]-[A6]).

These ideas are hardly convincing to a modern reader, and certainly not original. When she comes to more personal views, however, she grows more interesting; the following passage fairly states the procedure she follows in translating the book:

But as the French do not value a plain suit without a garniture, they are not satisfied with the advantages they have, but confound their own language with needless repetitions and tautologies; and by a certain rhetorical figure, peculiar to themselves, employ twenty lines, to express what an Englishman would say with more ease and sense in five; and this is the great misfortune of translating French into English: if one endeavors to make it English standard, it is no translation. If one follows their flourishes and embroideries, it is worse than French tinsel. . . .

I have endeavored to give you the true meaning of the author, and have kept as near his words as was possible; I was necessitated to add a little in some places, otherwise the book could not have been understood.   ([A7]-[A7ᵛ])

The rest of the preface is an elaborate defense of the Copernican system, a defense based on the view that "the design of the Bible was not to instruct mankind in astronomy, geometry, or chronology, but in the law of God . . ." ([a1ᵛ]). She proceeds by showing that "the words of the Scriptures favor one opinion as much as the other" ([a5]), a method familiar to any reader of contemporary theology. And she concludes with the inevitable political allusion: "We live in an age, wherein many believe nothing contained in that holy book, [and] others turn it into ridicule. Some use it only for mischief, and as a foundation and ground for rebellion; some keep close to the literal sense, and others give the words of God only that meaning and sense that pleases their own humors, or suits best their present purpose and interest" ([a7ᵛ]).

VII Lycidus

Lycidus; or, The Lover in Fashion (1688) is an adaptation of Tallemant's sequel, or second voyage, to the Island of Love. Mrs. Behn's technique is similar to that she used for *The Voyage,* except that she retains Tallemant's prose for the narrative sections instead of translating it into couplets. Both poetry and prose are expanded, but the poetry follows the French more closely than did that of *The Voyage,* and much of the prose is quite literally rendered. Mrs. Behn's handling of the verse is especially interesting since she had to produce a good English poem while keeping the substance of the French. Her verse often goes beyond mere competence, as in the following farewell to love:

> Adieu, lui dis-je, Amour, mes plus chères délices,
> Toi qui fus autrefois mon espoir le plus doux,
> Toi que j'aimai toujours malgré tous mes supplices;
> Amynte ne veut plus de commerce entre nous.
>
> Après sa trahison, & si lâche, & si noire,
> Je veux que de mon coeur ses traits soient effacés;
> Mais je ne veux jamais bannir de ma mémoire
> Tous ces heureux momens qu'avec toi j'ai passés.[9]

> Farewell, my little charming boy,
>   Farewell, my fond delight;
> My dear instructor all the day,
>   My soft repose at night.
> Thou, whom my soul has so caressed,
>   And my poor heart has held so fast;
> Thou never left me in my pain,
>   Nor in my happier hours;

> Thou eased me when I did complain,
>   And dried my falling showers.
> When Silvia frowned still thou wouldst smile,
>   And all my cares and griefs beguile.
>
> But Silvia's gone, and I have torn
>   Her witchcrafts from my heart,
> And nobly fortified by scorn
>   Her empire will subvert;
> Thy laws established there destroy,
>   And bid adieu to the dear charming boy.   (p.19)

The change in the second stanza is quite deliberate; the sentimentality that Tallemant has Tyrcis indulge in contradicts his character. In fact, Mrs. Behn improves the entire work by changing the narrator to avoid an even worse psychological inconsistency. Tallemant has Tyrcis tell the story of both voyages to his friend Lycidus. In the second, however, Tyrcis suddenly becomes the popular gallant pursuing, with cool command of the situation, two equally charming girls. In order to explain the sudden change of character, Tallemant revives Amynta and has her prove false. This betrayal causes Tyrcis to resolve never to be wounded again and motivates the casual pursuit of Sylvia and Iris. Mrs. Behn avoids the clumsy resurrection by having Lycidus make the second voyage on his friend's recommendation. His different experiences motivate his different attitude toward love: The falseness of Amynta is replaced by that of Sylvia, while Tallemant's Sylvia and Iris become Mrs. Behn's Bellimante and Bellinda. From this relatively early point on, the French is closely followed.

VIII   *"Of Trees"*

The last of Mrs. Behn's translations, like the first, is from the Latin. Abraham Cowley's *Sex libri plantarum* was first published in 1668, shortly after his death, in *Poemata latina*. A second edition appeared ten years later, and the moderate success of the work, Cowley's popularity in the Restoration, and perhaps a laudable desire for completeness, led the publishers of his works to put out *The Third Part of the Works of Mr. Abraham Cowley, Being His Six Books of Plants* . . . in 1689.

The translation was the work of several hands: "J. O." did books I and II; C. Cleve, Book III; and Nahum Tate, IV and V. Aphra Behn had always admired Cowley, but one may reasonably guess that her friend Tate got her the job of translating Book VI, "Of Trees," for this edition.

The task was a substantial one—her version comes to some 1750 lines—and she must often have regretted her scant knowledge of Latin. Furnished probably with a prose transliteration, she nevertheless produced an eminently readable and interesting poem, one nearly three-fourths again as long as the original. The lines on the beech tree, for example, illustrate her technique very well, and easily bear comparison with Cowley's own:

> Hinc olim juvenis mundi melioribus annis
> Fortunatarum domuum non magna supellex
> Tota petebatur; sellas, armaria, lectos,
> Et mensas dabat, et lances, et pocula fagus.
> His celebrare epulum veteres et festa solebant
> Vina coronati divis libare benignis,
> His retinere (opus haud fuerat placare) faventes.
> Nulla scyphos unquam infamarunt toxica tales:
> Sed sitis exhausit plenos secura, nec illud
> Arcanâ evenit ligni virtute potentis.
> Paupertas fuit antidotum contra omne venenum.[10]

> When first the infant-world her reign began,
> Ere pride and luxury had corrupted man,
> Before for gold the earth they did invade,
> The useful household-stuff of beech was made;
> No other plate the humble sideboard dressed,
> No other bowls adorned the wholesome feast,
> Which no voluptuous cookery could boast:
> The home-bred kid or lamb was all the cost;
> The mirth, the innocence, and little care,
> Surpassed the loaded boards of high-prized fare.
> There came no guest for interest or design,
> For guilty love, fine eating, or rich wine.
> The beechen bowl without debauch went round.
> And was with harmless mirth and roses crowned . . . (p.138)

If this passage, with its golden-age sentiments, was congenial to Mrs. Behn, the account of the oak must have been even more

so. Her Toryism matched Cowley's, and the political sentiments
which take up such a large part of the sixth book could hardly
have found a more willing proponent. One interpolation she
permitted herself, carefully indicating in the margin that "the
translatress in her own person speaks." The addition is to the
passage on the laurel and those who wear it:

> Among that number, do not me disdain,
> Me, the most humble of that glorious train.
> I by a double right thy bounties claim,
> Both from my sex, and in Apollo's name:
> Let me with Sappho and Orinda be
> O ever, sacred nymph, adorned by thee;
> And give my verses immortality.

In great pain and very near death, she could not resist pleading
for something time has at least partially granted her.

CHAPTER 8

The Novelist

MOST of Aphra Behn's fiction belongs to the last few years of her life and, like the translations, was probably produced as a quick source of income. Eight of her stories did not appear until after her death; the other five were published in 1688 and 1689. Of the group, only two can be shown from internal evidence to antedate 1685.

I Love Letters between a Nobleman and His Sister

Her first venture was not a story in the usual sense, but a fictionalized account of a contemporary scandal. Forde Grey, Lord Grey of Werk, was a strong Whig and supporter of the Exclusion Bill in the debates of 1681. He had married Mary, daughter of George, Lord Berkeley; but in 1682 he eloped with her sister Henrietta. The Tories succeeded in bringing him to trial in November on a charge of conspiracy, and he appeared in court not only with Lady Henrietta but also with several powerful figures among the Whig nobility. He was found guilty, and a fight ensued when Lord Berkeley tried to claim his daughter. Grey's later career, at least until the Revolution, was equally notorious. He was a party to the Rye House plot, and he escaped to Holland only to join with Monmouth in the latter's foolish plan for seizing the crown. Grey played a cowardly part in Monmouth's invasion but escaped punishment by turning informer. *Love Letters between a Nobleman and His Sister*, which Mrs. Behn published in 1684, includes a thinly disguised version of these notorious incidents. The form and style of the work derive from the famous *Portuguese Letters* of Guilleraques (1669), which proved extremely popular in England, and were often translated and imitated.[1]

Mrs. Behn's book is divided into three parts. The first, entirely epistolary, consists of fifty-seven letters of varying length.

They tell a story set during the rebellion of the Huguenots under Cesario, prince of Condé. Philander, an associate, falls in love with the prince's ex-mistress Myrtilla, carries her off with her consent, and marries her. But, quickly tiring of her and thinking she deceives him with Cesario, he soon falls in love with her sister Sylvia. Sylvia is, or pretends to be, an innocent; he seduces her, and they elope to St. Denis. They are discovered; and, to be free of her parents, she marries a tool of Philander, though the lad is to be husband in name only. The Huguenots are defeated and Philander imprisoned, but he escapes abroad with her. The letters are "found" later at St. Denis and "are as exactly as possible placed in the order they were sent, and were those supposed to be written towards the latter end of their amours."[2]

The key to the story is fairly obvious. Cesario is Monmouth; the Huguenot rebellion, the Rye House Plot; Philander, Myrtilla and Sylvia are Grey, his wife, and his mistress. The events are followed rather closely, though the pseudo-passionate style dictates long excursions on such themes as love versus honor and on such events as Sylvia's seduction. The popular appeal of such material is obvious, especially since Mrs. Behn was apparently fairly successful in passing the letters off as genuine.[3] Her motives must surely have included a political one; in the introduction, for example, she admits having "added a word or two" to Cesario's character in order to "render it a little more parallel to that of a modern prince in our age" (Sig. A2).

The second part of the book mixes narration with some thirty-four additional letters, and continues the story. In Holland the lovers meet Octavio, who falls in love with Sylvia in her disguise as a boy. She makes some female conquests to further titillate the reader, but eventually illness forces her to admit her sex and to tell their story. Octavio, a leading political figure, tells Philander he must leave but that he will take care of Sylvia until she can travel. Philander leaves, and soon justifies his name by another love intrigue, telling Brilliard (Sylvia's husband in name only) to keep her away for a while. Octavio pursues her avidly and makes an impression: "I must needs confess, Octavio, there is great eloquence in a pair of bracelets of five thousand crowns" (p. 200). She attempts to make Philander jealous by having Octavio write him about his passion, but the husband encourages him in a letter that might have been penned by the Rover himself: "I scour along the flowery plains of love, view all the charming prospect at a distance, which represents itself all gay and glorious!" (p. 214).

Philander also reveals that his new love is Calista, who turns out to be Octavio's sister and who is married to old Count Clarineau. Octavio's friendship with Philander does not permit him to show Sylvia Philander's letter, even to advance his prospects; but Philander soon writes her himself. She tries to stab herself, but her maid persuades her that "love and interest always do best together" (p. 234), a maxim she does not again forget. After an intrigue as complicated as any in the comedies and instigated by Brilliard in an attempt to gain Sylvia for himself, misunderstandings are cleared up. The now pregnant Sylvia agrees to marry Octavio merely to gain revenge on Philander, who has by now successfully seduced Calista.

Here Part II ends. It is obviously entirely fictional and without relation either to Lord Grey or to contemporary politics. Mrs. Behn's love of romantic intrigue, temporarily frustrated of its normal outlet in drama, is given full rein. The epistolary form, required in the *roman à clef* section of the work to maintain the pretence of authenticity, was obviously not suited to her wishes. More than half of Part II is narrated, though the letters are skillfully used even in the purely farcical section.

In Part III, originally published in 1687 as *The Amours of Philander and Sylvia,* Brilliard is told of Octavio's success, and in jealousy plots his arrest as a traitor. At the trial, Brilliard reveals he is married to Sylvia, but is not believed; eventually she confesses to Octavio, and after some delay on his part becomes his mistress. Fictional probability vanishes in an instant; he forgets business, fame, and honor while she spends his money everywhere. Under threat of disinheritance, he introduces Sylvia to his uncle. The uncle falls instantly in love with her and carries her off; Octavio follows and accidentally kills him. The two flee, but Octavio's estates are forfeit to the government. At this point Mrs. Behn remembers Philander and devotes the story to him. His success with Calista has resulted in her pregnancy, and they plan to elope. The escape ends in a fight and their capture; Calista escapes to a Brussels nunnery, where Sylvia visits her and tells her of Philander's past. As a result, Calista puts her baby out for adoption, takes "the habit, and remains a rare example of repentance and holy living" (p. 88).

In the remainder of the story, Cesario and the political situation are brought back: pardoned once, Cesario intrigues again and again against the king while engaging in a complicated amour with Hermione on the side. Philander reappears to contend at length with Octavio for Sylvia, and even Brilliard finally has his day. Eventually the disillusioned Octavio takes orders and retires to a monastery, happy at last and deaf to all appeals: "I have done with all the gilded vanities of life" (p. 175). Alonzo, a new character who appears to join the cabal, intrigues with Sylvia while using the Scot Fergusano to help incite Cesario to make the ill-starred invasion of his homeland. He is of course defeated. Philander and Cesario behave just as did Grey and Monmouth: Philander is pardoned, Fergusano escapes, Cesario dies on the block. The rest is fiction: Hermione starves to death of grief; Sylvia and Brilliard bilk Alonzo of his fortune and are thrown out of the country.

Part III is much more like a novel than Parts I or II. It includes eight letters, but more than nine-tenths is told by a first-person narrator who pretends to be an eyewitness of some of the events and a confidant of those who witnessed most of the rest. This attempt to achieve the authenticity of a true narrative, while by no means unique, deserves more attention than historians of fiction have given it. The attempt goes back to the dedication of Part I, where the author tells of a trip to Paris "last spring" during which she "met with a little book of letters, called, *L'Intrigue de Philander et Sylvia*" (A2). The story about finding the letters of Part I is another step, maintained in a later aside to one of them: "found torn in pieces" (p. 61). The epistolary form inhibits such comments, and Mrs. Behn often strains the reader's belief in another direction: the reader must know how Philander escapes from Sylvia's bedroom, but it is a little disturbing to have him telling her how he did it in a letter written some time later.

The addition of a narrator in Part II makes the task easier. The narrator is used to summarize the action, to describe and make judgments about the characters, and more than once to attest the truth of the whole story. These techniques are even more common in Part III. When Calista first learns of Philander's past, a nun comes in "whom I have since heard protest, she scarcely saw in that moment any alteration in her" (p. 87). The best example occurs at the ordination of Octavio. The narrator has not only been to the monastery, but attends the ceremony in person: "I confess, I thought myself no longer on earth; and sure there is nothing gives an idea of real heaven, like a church all adorned . . ." (p. 179). The description is detailed, lengthy, and quite convincing; at one point Octavio "came near me, to be welcomed by a father that sat next to me" (p. 182); and the narrator admits to nearly swooning. The real events which figure in Part III are skillfully used to establish the credibility of the romance as well. If "all historians agree" that Philander did not desert Cesario for want of courage (p. 253), the public is more likely to believe in his amours as well. And, indeed, the romance is hardly more incredible than most of the history.

The characterization of Sylvia which develops during the three parts is a very skillful one. She begins as an innocent, but character and events make her an accomplished and pleasure-seeking woman whose only interests in life are excitement, sex, and personal comfort. At first she talks of love having "quite confounded nature" in her (I, 118), but the narrator later shows, as well as tells, us that "she had not a heart that any love, or loss of honor, or fortune could break" (III, 147). The analysis is occasionally penetrating: when Sylvia is trying to win back Philander, he makes her contract to submit entirely to his wishes. She accepts, and the narrator remarks that "she bends like a slave for a little empire over him" (III, 155).

Love Letters, though almost unknown today, is Mrs. Behn's longest fictional work,[4] comprising more than a third of the pages she devoted to this genre. It is interesting not only for the characterization of Sylvia and its treatment of contemporary politics, but as the work in which Mrs. Behn made the transition between romantic and intrigue drama on the one hand and the quite different requirements of fiction on the other. From her dramatic career, she knew the necessity for keeping things moving, the advantages of dialogue, and the importance of

self-characterization. Fiction offered her at least equal opportunities for complication and intrigue and, through the narrator,
an increased scope in terms of both space and time. The style
of *Love Letters* is hardly more inflated or turgid than that of
Samuel Richardson's *Pamela* (1740), but Mrs. Behn lacks his
ability to sustain a psychological analysis within a simple and
unified structure.

II *"The Court of the King of Bantam"*

Two stories which were first published in 1698(?) were also
written during this period. The first, titled "The Court of the
King of Bantam," may be dated rather precisely from internal
evidence. A concert entertains the company "with the best and
newest airs in the last new plays, being then in the year 1683"
(p. 17).[5] Later Friendly invites Would-be King to see *The
London Cuckolds*, first produced in 1682; and the narrator
wryly remarks, "I don't hear that his Majesty, King Charles the
Second, ever sent any ambassador" even though the King "is a
wonderful . . . gentleman" (p. 26). With the certainty of a date
between 1682 and the death of Charles in February, 1685, the
reference to 1683 strongly suggests that the story was written in
1684.

"The King of Bantam" is told in first person by a narrator
purporting to be a close friend of the heroine. The plot is built
upon the trick Sir Philip Friendly plays on the fantastic Would-
be King during Twelfth-Night festivities. This wealthy gull,
who fancies himself a monarch, is chosen by lot to be King of
Bantam. Valentine Goodland loves Philibella, Sir Philip's niece;
and the company tricks Would-be into giving her the necessary
dowry as payment for her help in gaining him a night with her
sister Queen Lucy, who turns out to be Sir Philip's discarded
mistress in disguise. The love story is subservient to the trick,
which is recounted with considerable gusto and also with a
great many realistic details. The style, in fact, is atypical; an
advertisement to the 1698 edition to the *Histories and Novels*
informs the reader that "it was a trial of skill upon a wager, to
shew that she was able to write in the style of the celebrated
Scarron, in imitation of whom 'tis writ, though the story be
true."[6]

The tale begins abruptly and informally: "This money, certainly, is a most devilish thing! I'm sure the want of it had like to have ruined my dear Philibella . . ." (p. 13). And though the characters have stock names, we are told exactly how much money Sir Philip's wife's first husband left her and that he lived after their marriage "let me see—in the Strand; or, as near as I can remember, somewhere about Charing Cross" (p. 442). The Christmas setting is specific, even to the claret, roasted oranges, and cake; the stakes of the card game are mentioned, as is the time of the play, the taverns visited, and the streets through which the company passes. The narrator makes every effort to establish the story, even to the clever disclaimer put in before the last few facts are told: "The rest I have forgot" (p. 33). The result is amusing and well written, but Would-be is pretty improbable even for a fool.

III   "The Unfortunate Happy Lady"

The second story in this group, "The Unfortunate Happy Lady: A True History," may also be dated from internal references. Philadelphia, the heroine, is besieged by as many lovers "as our dear King Charles, whom God grant long to reign, was lately by the Presbyterians . . . and all those canting Whiggish brethren" (p. 59). This statement suggests Whig activities against the Catholics between the Exclusion Bill and the Rye House Plot (1681-83), and it gives a terminal date of February, 1685. Again, 1684 is a likely date.

The story itself is a romance with many realistic details. It begins with a distant echo of *The Miseries of Enforced Marriage*. The profligate Sir William Wilding inherits his estate and spends it all in riot, including the six thousand pounds due his sister Philadelphia. To avoid her claim on him, he tries to turn her into a prostitute by tricking her into lodging with a bawd. She is saved by Gracelove, the man who pays to seduce her; affected by her story, he gets her lodgings with his friend Fairlaw's family and wins her hand. Before they can be married, he is presumed lost at sea. After grieving for several years, she marries Fairlaw upon the death of his wife, but she soon becomes a widow. Sir William meanwhile goes from bad to worse, but she eventually redeems him from debtor's prison, pays off all of his debts, and marries him to Fairlaw's daughter Eugenia. She also finds Gracelove, acts as his fairy godmother, and finally marries him.

Woodcock calls the tale "an involved story told with masterly conciseness,"[7] and at least the first half of his statement is beyond dispute. But such a crude and disjointed story can hardly be considered as concise in the usual sense of the word. Sir William begins strongly, but fades out after a few pages. Then come the scenes at old Beldam's, then Philadelphia's career after Gracelove's departure, and finally her actions as fairy godmother. The story is really a string of rather disparate episodes spread out over a wide time span by inadequate narrative summarizing and unified only by the presence of Philadelphia. As such, it is one of the weakest of Mrs. Behn's stories.

IV The Fair Jilt

The Fair Jilt; or, The History of Prince Tarquin and Miranda, published in 1688, is a much more ambitious work.[8] Held together by Mrs. Behn's philosophy of love and her careful focus on a single character, it is an interesting study of the *femme fatale* theme. The rich and beautiful Miranda ruins one man after another, both before and after her marriage to Prince Tarquin. She falls in love with a friar and, in revenge for his fidelity to his vows, has him imprisoned on a charge of rape. She leads her page to attempt the murder of her sister; on the day of his execution, he apologizes for his weakness in accusing one so lovely. Tarquin's wealth is squandered and he himself reduced to attempted murder, yet he loves her still; on the block he announces his satisfaction in dying in her service. Redeemed by an inept executioner, he escapes only to have her join him in retirement in Holland.

The story falls into two parts. After a leisurely introduction, emphasizing the all-conquering power of love and presenting the heroine, Cornelia relates the story of Friar Henrick and the sequence of events leading to his rejection of her. In this part of the story, used to establish Miranda's personality, the first-person narrator describes her as "naturally amorous, but extremely inconstant" (pp. 13-14). Soon it is clear that she is amoral—incapable even of understanding a moral code independent of her own immediate desires. She cannot conceive, when Henrick rejects her, that his devotion to religion can be real: "for a little hypocritical devotion," she says, "you resolve to lose the greatest blessings of life, and to sacrifice me to your religious pride and vanity . . ." (p. 49).

The second part of the story centers on her relationship with Prince Tarquin. He represents the perfect man and lover—rich, noble, handsome, and the soul of honor. Their amour exemplifies the fatal power of love: Tarquin is ruined morally and financially by a destructive and irrational attraction which he recognizes yet embraces gladly. It is no small tribute to Mrs. Behn's skill that both the prince and Miranda remain believable, at least until the quite conventional ending.

The Fair Jilt, like most of Mrs. Behn's fiction, is presented as essentially true. She attests to this in the dedication to Henry Pain, Esq. Hundreds know the prince's story, she says, including Pain; she was a witness to those parts of it that Tarquin himself did not relate to her. Later she says that what she did not see "was confirmed of by actors in the intrigue, holy men, of the Order of St. Francis . . ." (p. 7). Even the history of Prince Henrick was told Cornelia by her brother, who "was an officer under the prince, his father" (p. 32). When the narrator must refer to the contents of a letter, she says she was told them by Henrick himself (p. 42); when Tarquin is introduced, she begins "We had often heard of this great man . . ." (p. 59). Later she refers to a time "which I have not been so curious as to retain, or put in my journal observations" (p. 87).

The "historical" character of the narrative is maintained not only by these assertions but by the wealth of circumstantial detail. Tarquin's journey to the block is complete even to the color of the hinges on his coffin. Place names are frequently given, and so are amounts of money and periods of time. As a final touch, the narrator knows events beyond the limits of her tale: Henrick "is yet living in Antwerp" (p. 104), and "since I began this relation, I heard that Prince Tarquin died about three-quarters of a year ago" (p. 120).

Defoe comes immediately to mind in reading *The Fair Jilt;* he did not originate the technique of "circumstantial detail" for which he is best known, but merely refined and extended it.

The difficulty Mrs. Behn has comes from trying to fit an essentially romantic story into a realistic mold; *Moll Flanders* is often improbable, but it is not romantic, and therefore it is more successful. Montague Summers asserts that "the history is mainly true" (p. 69), but his remark only attests his enthusiasm for his subject. Miranda comes alive as a fictional creation, but the story as a whole has far too many analogues in European literature to warrant searching Holland for Tarquin's genealogy.[9]

V   Oronooko

Oronooko; or, The Royal Slave, labeled *A True History,* appeared shortly after *The Fair Jilt.*[10] It is the one work of fiction which preserves the name of Aphra Behn to the modern reader, partly because of its intrinsic merit and partly because of its influence on subsequent literary history. Many of her plays are finer works than this story, but none is more original or has been so widely printed or so widely read.

The plot is relatively simple. Oronooko, prince of Coramantien and the type of heroism and beauty, falls in love with Imoinda. The king, his grandfather, takes her for his harem and, after Oronooko nevertheless manages to consummate their love, has her sold into slavery. Soon after, Oronooko and many of his followers are tricked by a slave trader and sold to the English planters at Surinam; his noble character, however, wins him partial freedom. He is reunited with Imoinda, whom he thought dead, and promised his complete freedom. When Imoinda becomes pregnant, he grows suspicious of the colonists' assurances and leads an abortive revolt to establish his own colony. Deserted by his fellow slaves, he is tortured by the treacherous Byam and vows revenge. Knowing her fate if he fails, he kills Imoinda; but he is so overcome by grief that he lies eight days in a stupor. The members of council approach him; he rips himself open in contempt of anything they can do; but is rescued by friends of the narrator. His wounds are mortal; but before he dies, the vicious Byam seizes him, tortures him, and burns him at the stake.

Like *The Fair Jilt, Oronooko* has a two-part structure. The events in Coramantien introduce him and Imoinda, establish their love and his valor, intelligence, and nobility of character.

The events in Surinam show him a prisoner in a world controlled by cruel, venal men whose cowardice and treachery succeed by virtue of their numbers. The result goes beyond pathos to tragedy. Charismatic in his own world, Oronooko is inevitably feared by a society of inferiors. The organization is better handled in the novel than in the preceding tale. No inset story mars the continuity of narration; the focus does not slip from one relationship to another but remains on Oronooko himself throughout. Little is made of the contrast between the friar and Prince Tarquin, but much is made of the contrast between Coramantien and Surinam.

The structural unity of *Oronooko* is unusual in fiction of its time, and its thematic unity is even more so. Mrs. Behn ironically juxtaposes two orders of life and manipulates them with great skill. The two orders have certain features in common: warfare and slavery are sanctioned in both; Oronooko sells those he conquers in battle and Surinam buys. Some of the evils associated with power are also present in both: Oronooko's grandfather takes Imoinda from him; Byam also misuses his authority, though for less excusable purposes. But at the heart of the story is the contrast between the nobility of the supposedly savage Oronooko and the baseness of the supposedly civilized English colonists. Oronooko wins his captives in battle, but he is himself captured by treachery. He is a man of his word, a man to whom honor is more sacred than life; the colonists are constant in deceit. He kills fairly; they torture and mutilate. He is capable of a love they can only wonder at; they of dishonor which at first is beyond his comprehension.

Part of the irony is obvious: he is the civilized man; they, the savages. But *Oronooko* is not primarily a document in the history of romantic primitivism. The true primitives in the story are the native Indians; their unlikely innocence and virtue ally the story to this tradition far more than the figures in the main plot. In fact, Mrs. Behn takes some pains to inform the reader that Oronooko has been educated in European mores and values through his French tutor and numerous conversations with visiting traders. He is thus not a true savage, nor is his nobility inherent.

In fact, Oronooko functions in the story as an embodiment of just those values affirmed by European societies under the

The Novelist

influence of Christianity and the humanistic tradition. "He had nothing of barbarity in his nature, but in all points addressed himself as if his education had been in some European court" (p. 19). Thus the fundamental irony of the tale comes from the confrontation of society by its own ideal; the tragedy derives from the inability of that society to tolerate the burden of its guilt. The point is sharpened by the attitude of the prince to the gods of the "Christians" in the story: "Farewell, Sir, 'tis worth my suffering to gain so true a knowledge, both of you and of your gods, by whom you swear" (p. 149). The closest analogy here is not between *Oronooko* and Jean Jacques Rousseau's *La nouvelle Héloise* but between Mrs. Behn's story and a tale like Mary Shelley's *Frankenstein:* if the doctor's creation may be seen as the projection of the guilt and evil within man, Mrs. Behn's may be seen as the projection of the ideals man sets himself.

In one other respect this story surpasses its predecessors. Ernest Baker aptly notes the "bareness" of her earlier stories and the more elaborate setting of this one.[11] The exotic description, some perhaps based on memory, some probably taken from George Warren's *An Impartial Description of Surinam*,[12] defines the action in place and time and adds greatly to the credibility of the action. Much of the description, to be sure, is troweled in like mortar between the bricks of the story, but the details, even though they are crudely handled, help bring the story to life. Some even have a thematic function: Oronooko holds his own with the half-mythical tiger, but not with the all too realistic colonists, who long ago had left one jungle for another.[13]

Oronooko had a topical interest derived from its setting in a colony recently lost to the Dutch, and for most subsequent readers has had a strong biographical appeal as well. Both are quite irrelevant to the story as art, since what matters is not whether Mrs. Behn was or was not in Surinam, or whether she knew Oronooko or created him, but how well she establishes the illusion of truth by the narrative devices she uses. By some tests she is successful. The constant claims of the narrator to personal knowledge of the characters and events of the story carry more conviction than similar assertions in previous stories, and her success is a consequence of her more assured technique in handling the historical pose. The casual reference to "one Banister" (p. 236) and the allusions to "my mother and sister" (p. 238) and "my new comedy" (p. 209) are good examples.

In other respects the story is less successful. The romance between Oronooko and Imoinda—indeed, everything about that young lady—comes from the heroic tradition, probably through the English heroic drama and the French Arcadian romance. The love story has tangential relevance to the theme, but it belongs to a rather different kind of fiction. It causes the awkward resolution of the story: Oronooko as an ideal hero must not execute the revenge he naturally desires, yet his honor and prowess must not be questioned. The romantic tradition provides a solution, and in effect he dies of grief. But his grief is self-inflicted as a necessary step to revenge, and Mrs. Behn cannot quite solve the dilemma she creates by having Imoinda's death justified only by action she cannot permit Oronooko to take.

The technical weaknesses in the handling of setting and theme, especially since little fiction of the period is free from them, do not keep *Oronooko* from being one of the best pieces of seventeenth-century English fiction. John Bunyan's *Pilgrim's Progress* of course surpasses it, but that work belongs to a radically different mode. Defoe was to achieve in his novels a technical control of detail beyond Mrs. Behn's, but the control of point of view successfully maintained in *Oronooko* contrasts sharply with the spurious moral pose of the narrator of *Moll Flanders*. Moreover, Mrs. Behn invests her story with a thematic significance that does not appear again before Richardson and Fielding.

VI Agnes de Castro

The last of the three stories published in 1688, *Agnes de Castro*, is an adaptation of Mlle de Brillac's *Agnes de Castro, nouvelle Portugaise* (1688). The French work, in turn, is a version of a story well known in European literature.[14] When Dona Constança Manuel was married to Dom Pedro, prince of Portugal, she took with her to Affonso IV's court her beautiful relative Inês de Castro. Pedro and Inês immediately fell in love; he married her secretly upon the death of Constança in 1345, after she had borne him several children. The king, learning of the marriage, had Inês killed in Pedro's absence, starting a civil war which ended only with Affonso's death in 1357. Mrs. Behn's version of the story follows Mlle de Brillac's fairly closely. Constantia loves Pedro and Agnes; Agnes loves Constantia and is indifferent to Pedro until his wife's death. Elvira Gonzales and her brother Don Alvaro are the villains, the one arousing a fatal jealousy in Constantia, the other pressing the king until he consents to Agnes' assassination.

The story is much inferior to *The Fair Jilt* and *Oronooko*, the other two stories of this year, collected with it under the title *Three Histories* a little after first publication. What interest it has centers on the conflict between love and honor in Pedro, and the rather incredible ability of Constantia to love both her husband and her unwitting rival. The emotional stops are pulled out, but Agnes' death is pathetic rather than tragic. The characters are too wooden, and the story is too short to permit sufficient development of them. Their emotions come out of the love versus honor convention rather than out of concrete and detailed presentation. The announced theme—the irresistible and irrational power of love—is similar to that of *The Fair Jilt*. Tarquin, however, engages in a number of specific actions and in numerous conversations; Pedro, on the other hand, is presented largely from the outside. Agnes talks more than Miranda, but the nature of the plot allows her no action, and she is never a realized figure. The theme possibly drew Mrs. Behn to the story, but her original treatments of the fatal power of love are clearly superior.

VII *The History of the Nun*

Mrs. Behn's next tale, published in 1689 as *The History of the Nun; or, The Fair Vow-Breaker*, is a romance masquerading as an exemplum. The young and beautiful Isabella takes the vows of a nun, then falls in love with Henault and breaks her vows to elope with him. The Church forgives, but Henault's father will relent only if his son achieves military glory. Villenoys, an earlier lover, brings Isabella news of Henault's death in battle and eventually marries the widow. But Henault was not killed, and he returns after eight years to claim his wife. Isabella, now loving the wealthy Villenoys, smothers Henault and tells Villenoys that he died upon learning of her remarriage. The faithful husband promises to throw the body in the river, but Isabella sews the sack to his coat and thus insures his death as well. Confronted by a Frenchman who knew Henault in captivity, she confesses all and is executed.

Both the narrator and Isabella insist that the catastrophe arises as a result of the nun's broken vows. Isabella's last words, in fact, are a sermon to the crowd on the exemplary nature of her own life. But the narrator also insists throughout on the inability of men and women to resist the force of passionate love: Isabella is a very saint until subjected to love's power, and in all actions not connected with love she remains so until her death. The moral the story presents is thus spurious and imposed—a mere excuse for a romantic and improbable tale. The rarefied atmosphere and basic situation come from *Love Letters of a Nun to a Cavalier* and the whole popular tradition engendered by the Guilleraques story, while the action has probably as many analogues as that of *Agnes de Castro*.

The inadequacy of the story is best shown by an analysis of its structure. The first part introduces the moral issue and sees Isabella reject Villenoys and her other suitors for the nunnery. Then comes the romance with Henault, a section devoted to long passages setting forth the choice between Isabella's vows and her passion, and the inevitable success of the latter. The third section resurrects Villenoys and supposedly buries Henault; it culminates in Isabella's second marriage. The fourth sees the return of Henault and the murder of both husbands; the fifth, Isabella's discovery and execution. Even a rapid reading of the story reveals the inadequacy of the last two parts. Isabella's power over her lovers is presented as immense, yet she fears Henault will subject her to poverty and shame by insisting on her return to him. (Tennyson was here perhaps more realistic: Enoch Arden walks into the sunset.) And Mrs. Behn's conclusion is even worse. The Frenchman is an obvious *deus ex machina* to save the moral: the natural end of the story would see Isabella live ever after with Villenoys, though perhaps not quite happily. Guilt drives her to confess, but nothing very satisfactory drives her to the fatal stitches on her husband's coat.

The structural failure, the rapid conclusion, and the spurious moral all suggest that Mrs. Behn has no real focus in the story. Great attention is given to the conflict in Isabella's mind even though its outcome is foreordained. On the other hand, she murders twice after hardly a paragraph of analysis, and until that point is never revealed as suffering any qualms of conscience about her choice. The story might have been a fascinating study of the degeneration of character under the pressure of guilt, but the author turns it instead into a crime narrative with a tacked-on moral. Parts of it are interesting; the handling of the young Isabella's rejection of the world, for example, is superbly done. The reader respects the sincerity of her vows though aware of how ephemeral they will prove; and Henault's success becomes a logical step. But such achievements do not redeem the tale as a whole, and it is difficult to see why it has been called "a quite remarkable study in the psychology of crime and guilt."[15]

VIII The Lucky Mistake

The Lucky Mistake, also published in 1689, contains in its dedication the customary disclaimer: The story is "not translation but an original, that has more of reality than fiction; if I have not made it fuller of intrigue, 'twas because I had a mind to keep close to the truth." But the narrator makes no more attempt in this story than in *Agnes de Castro* or *The History of the Nun* to establish this truth during the course of the story; these stories are thereby differentiated from *Oronooko* and *The Fair Jilt.* Mrs. Behn rightly sub-titles her story a novel: *The Lucky Mistake* is a conventional romance with a happy ending. Renaldo and Atlante, like Romeo and Juliet, are young neighbors whose love is opposed by their parents. Vernole, who wants Atlante for himself, is the villain who abandons his evil role in the last act. He is rewarded with Atlante's sister Charlot, a brisk and outspoken girl who, the reader feels, has escaped the convent for a not much better fate.

The story is pleasant and unpretentious. Mrs. Behn succeeds in maintaining an evenly paced narrative, with only the unprepared metamorphosis of Vernole to spoil the effect. The emphasis, as in most of her intrigue comedies, is on the plot.

This focus makes *The Lucky Mistake* simpler and more successful technically, but also less interesting than *The Fair Jilt* or *The History of the Nun*. Where the plot, characters, and narrative devices are conventional, and the style no more than adequate, there is little to hold the reader for long.

IX "The Nun"

"The Nun; or, the Perjured Beauty," first published in the 1698(?) edition of the *Histories and Novels*, is even less interesting. In the matter-of-fact opening of the tale, Antonio saves his friend Henrique from death at the hand of Sebastian, whose sister Elvira has been abused by Henrique. Antonio, kept by their parents' feud from his loved Ardelia, persuades Henrique to pretend to court her in order to arrange an elopement. The convention of love versus honor is subsequently strained to the utmost. Henrique and Ardelia fall in love; in an orgy of masochism they renounce each other, but Ardelia soon tells Antonio all and the honorable Henrique is forced to kill his friend in a duel. Ardelia, seemingly overcome by guilt, takes the veil but soon repents of her vows: when Sebastian comes to seek his revenge, she falls in love with him. Elvira warns Henrique of their intended elopement, and at the appointed hour the rivals kill each other after Sebastian accidentally runs Ardelia through with his sword. Elvira obligingly dies of fever and grief; and the narrator, having killed off all the characters, must bring the story to a close.

Ardelia is another of the fickle heroines who illustrate the fatal power of love. Like Sylvia, Miranda, and Isabella, she is young and beautful; like them, she inspires instantly a passion no man can resist. But in this story she is merely roughed in by the narrator; her inconstancy, for example, is completely unmotivated. She is the excuse for a love-against-friendship debate between two other unrealized abstractions, and the source of the moral—no more. She offers neither the vividness and interest attached to Sylvia and Miranda, nor the occasional psychological probing shown in the portrayal of Isabella. No amount of Mrs. Behn's highly inflated rhetoric can make either her fate or that of her lovers interesting or significant. The story is one more *novella* of adventure and blood, tricked out with pseudo-philosophical debate and spiced by the indirect sex of the *Portuguese Letters.*

X *"The Adventure of the Black Lady"*

The other story which first appeared in the 1698(?) edition is "The Adventure of the Black Lady."[16] It is hardly more than an anecdote: Bellamora is united to her lover Fondlove through a remarkable series of coincidences just before her baby is born. The story belongs to romance, but Mrs. Behn adds many specific details in an attempt to give her first-person narrative credibility, and tells the story in a matter of fact way far removed from the style of Guilleraques and of his translator Roger L'Estrange. The opening sentence demonstrates both features: "About the beginning of last June (as near as I can remember) Bellamora came to town from Hampshire, and was obliged to lodge the first night at the same inn where the stagecoach set up" (p. 3). The story moves quickly toward the lovers' inevitable reunion; everything but the spare style and the references to the overseers of the poor as "the vermin of the parish" (p. 9) might be found today in any ladies' magazine.

XI The Wandering Beauty

Mrs. Behn returns momentarily to the historical pose in *The Wandering Beauty* (1698), and she also touches on one of her favorite themes—the evil of enforced marriage. Exchanging clothes with a farmer's daughter, Arabella runs away to avoid old Sir Robert Richland. Two weeks of wandering bring her to Sir Christian Kindly's, where, under the delightful pseudonym of Peregrina Goodhouse, she attends his daughter Eleanora. After three happy years, she is sought in marriage by Sir Lucius Lovewell; and, in a wonderfully stylized scene, she accepts him with Kindly's blessing. Their marriage is ideal, but she longs for her parents and, with her husband's assistance, returns home for a happy reunion.

The story is a superb fairy tale, told in a simple and unpretentious style. Arabella is the beautiful princess who has to leave home but who is magically protected and loved by everyone she meets. Sir Christian's name announces his role; the daughter that Lovewell originally came to woo conveniently loves another man; Arabella's sisters are content with a smaller portion; Love-well's generosity in marrying a dowerless girl rejected by the parson is rewarded with ten thousand pounds and three thousand pounds per year; and even the peasant's daughter gets clothes beyond her dreams. No sentimentality mars the story, parts of which have a masque-like quality unique in Mrs. Behn's fiction. The setting, which is unusually detailed and specific, marks her first attempt to use the English countryside, which appears infrequently in fiction of her era.

XII   The Unfortunate Bride

The Unfortunate Bride; or, The Blind Lady a Beauty also first appeared in 1698. It is a peculiar story, beginning as a conventional romance between Frankwit and Belvira, with a suggestion of complication from the "inviolable" friendship the former has with Wildvill. As Frankwit spends his money in lavish courtship, the story enters the realm of the comedy of wit: "the young gallant washed himself clean of that shining dirt, his gold; he fancied little of heaven dwelt in his yellow angels, but let them fly away, as it were on their own golden wings" (p. 404). He and Belvira have a dialogue that might have been written by Congreve or spoken by the Rover, for it is full of witty images. But with the entrance of Moorea, the evil witch, the story takes a turn for the worse, and it ends up a conventional romantic tragedy with some plot borrowed from *The History of the Nun* and some from "The Nun; or, The Perjured Beauty." The blind lady of the title, who is miraculously cured, receives Frankwit from the dying Belvira in a final scene as sentimental as it is unconvincing.

XIII   The Dumb Virgin

The narrator enters the above story directly as the close friend of Belvira. But she functions not merely as a witness to the events of the tale but as an actor in them by sending the intercepted letters of the two lovers to Belvira just before Frankwit makes his fatal appearance. This stratagem is also used in *The Dumb Virgin; or, The Force of Imagination,* first published in 1700. The narrator is delighted at her chance to converse with one of the Venetian heroines (p. 424), and she is present at the great masquerade ball to meet the mysterious Englishman Dangerfield (p. 426). She lives "within three doors of Rinaldo's house" (p. 444), and thus she is enabled to see the tableau which ends the story and to be the recipient of Dangerfield's last words. The technique is interesting since it blurs the distinction between first- and third-person narration in an effort to achieve the illusion of history.

But the attempt is unsuccessful because the events belong to psychological rather than to objective history. The son of a Venetian senator, lost at sea as a baby, returns as an unknown English hero. Meeting his sisters Belvideera and Maria at a masquerade, he flirts with both; but he is challenged to a duel by jealous rivals. The fight is broken up by his father, who invites him home. There he falls in love with Maria and, through a series of improbable circumstances, seduces the congenitally speechless girl. As he is leaving, he is attacked by his rivals; and in the struggle he accidentally stabs his father and is mortally wounded himself. As the two are dying, the son's identity is revealed by a birthmark; when Maria understands that she is guilty of incest, she recovers the power of speech, reveals their crime, and stabs herself as her brother and father die.

As one of the hundreds of variants of the Oedipus myth, the story is inherently convincing as the embodiment of a common wish and the guilt attached to it. But it is not at all convincing as art. It is short, yet the plot is quite complicated; the sequence of events takes so much time to narrate that no focus on the characters or the meaning of the incest is attained. The reader is asked to accept this report as a true account, yet it makes use of one romance convention after another: the beautiful but deformed heroine, the identifying birthmark, love at first sight, the masquerade ball, the jealous rival, and so on. These conventions might possibly have been used to present the myth meaningfully, but they certainly oppose the devices used to achieve verisimilitude.

XIV   The Unhappy Mistake

Woodcock, following Baker, dismisses *The Unhappy Mistake; or, The Impious Vow Punished* (1700(?)) as "a hackneyed little tale on the old theme of a lover who works himself into a frenzy of jealousy because he sees his mistress in the arms of another man, who is really her brother."[17] His summary fairly represents the plot, in which Miles Hardyman is the son who is in love with Diana Constance, whose brother Lewis he thinks his rival. When Miles is prevented from marrying her by his father, who cannot overlook the inequality of their estates, he rejects his patrimony with a vow never to see Sir Henry again. After a duel Miles wins distinction as an officer in France, but in a few more years ends up a penniless soldier in London. There Lewis finds him; and, after a lengthy preparation very similar to that in "The Unfortunate Happy Lady," Mrs. Behn restores to him his estate, his mistress, and his dead father's title.

The plot does not indicate the interest of the story. For one thing, the setting is again English; and it is rather carefully detailed, particularly Miles's life in London after his exile. For another, the story contains excellent dialogue—the best, in fact, in Mrs. Behn's fiction. The discussion between Miles and his father about money is a good example: Sir Henry is a worthy if better educated ancestor of Fielding's Squire Western in *Tom Jones:*

Beauty and virtue, Sir, (returned young Hardyman) with the addition of good humor and education, is a dowry that may merit a crown. Notion! Stuff! All stuff (cried the old knight)! Money is beauty, virtue, good humor, education, reputation, and high birth. Thank Heaven, Sir, (said Miles) you don't live as if you believed your own doctrine; you part with your money very freely in your housekeeping, and I am happy to see it. 'Tis that I value it for (replied the father); I would therefore have thee, my son, add to what in all likelihood will be thine, so considerably, by marriage, that thou mayst better deserve the character of hospitable Hardyman than thy father Sir Henry.—Come, Miles (returned he), thou shalt think no more on her. I can't avoid it, Sir (said t'other). Well, well, think of her you may (said Sir Henry), but not as for a wife; no, if you mean to continue in your father's love, be not in love with Madam Diana, nor with any of her nymphs, though never so fair or so chaste—unless they have got store of money, store of money, Miles. Come, come in, we'll take a game at chess before dinner, if we can.   (p. 474)

Sir Henry's wrath at his son's departure and duel is also well done; and, until he quite improbably and uncharacteristically takes up the company of bats and owls and dies of grief, he is an excellent proof of Mrs. Behn's skill in comic portraiture.

Unfortunately, the public taste was for romantic melodrama, and Mrs. Behn never developed in her fiction the broadly comic realism so evident in many of her plays. The novels are often interesting, but *Oronooko* is the only one which can bear any comparison with her better plays and poems. She made no significant contribution to the development of the form, and even her role in the sentimental and primitivist movements has been exaggerated.

CHAPTER 9

Summing Up: Aphra Behn, 1689-1967

IN her own day, and through most of the eighteenth and nine-teenth centuries, Mrs. Behn was known primarily as a drama-tist. *The Rover* and *The Emperor of the Moon* were played well into the middle of the eighteenth century; and, except for commendatory verses, lampoons, and biographical notices, most of the early comment on her comes in the work of stage his-torians like Theophilus Cibber, Gerard Langbaine, Thomas Wilkes, Charles Dibden, John Genest, and John Doran. Her fiction was only tangentially relevant, as the source of the plots of such plays as Thomas Southerne's *Oronooko* (1694) and *The Fatal Marriage* (1696), or Mrs. Catherine Cockburn's *Agnes de Castro: A Tragedy* (1696).

As a dramatist, Mrs. Behn was both praised and attacked, but praise predominates: she was clearly considered by her contemporaries as a competent playwright of the second rank. Langbaine compared her to Katherine Philips,[1] and William Oldys noted her "ready command of pertinent expressions," her "pregnant and fluent" fancy, and her "facility, spirit, and warmth, especially in amorous subjects, superior to every other poetess of the age, and many of the poets too; so that none among us may, perhaps, more justly be called The English Sappho. . . ."[2]

The critics often complained of her many borrowings, but most of the adverse criticism concerns her personal morals and the supposed indecency of her plays. Pope's facile couplet in the Epistle to Augustus—"The stage how loosely does Astraea tread, / Who fairly puts all characters to bed"—is famous; and he is by no means alone in his allegation. Nevertheless, it is interesting that those who attack Mrs. Behn for obscenity are usually lampoonists or party hacks; one must emphasize again that her plays are not indecent by the standards of her age and that in her adaptations of earlier plays she invariably reduces or eliminates the indelicate language of the originals. Pope's comment is unfair, though clever; Dryden's remarks in a similar vein[3] came when, as an old man, his piety led him to reject the age of which his own comedies were a part. The Restoration drama has now largely freed itself from the two centuries of diatribe against its looseness, and Dr. Doran's judgment of Mrs. Behn as "a mere harlot, who danced through uncleanness,"[4] seems today not merely absurd but amusing.

Victorian reaction is well shown in the controversy surrounding Pearson's 1871 reprint of Mrs. Behn's works: the publisher put out a pamphlet citing commendatory verses and the early dramatic historians in her favor,[5] and the *Athenaeum* and the *Saturday Review* retaliated with remarks like "time has not staled the foulness of the ordure,"[6] and "She was . . . one of the original corrupters and polluters of the stage."[7] Julia Kavanagh had earlier suggested, rather naïvely, that her private life might have been pure,[8] but among nineteenth-century writers only Blake and Swinburne saw anything in her work to admire.

Attitudes began to change somewhat about the turn of the century, but serious articles like Paul Siegel's for *Anglia* in 1902[9] are quite rare. More common were general "appreciations," or depreciations like Paul Elmer More's,[10] provoked by Montague Summers' edition of 1915. But nearly everything written about Mrs. Behn is either biographical or concerned with the moral issue. The increasing interest in her fiction—largely brought about by Ernest A. Baker's reprint of most of her stories,[11] and by his well-known *History of the English Novel*— is probably as much due to the twentieth-century importance of this genre as to any real conviction that Mrs. Behn is a better novelist than dramatist. *Oronooko* is now better known than all of her plays together, but no one who reads her works attentively can fail to notice that its popularity does her reputation considerable injustice.

The post World War I period produced the first full-length treatments of Mrs. Behn. Victoria Sackville-West's *Aphra Behn*

(1928) dealt almost exclusively with biography and primarily with the Surinam and Antwerp episodes—as did the Jerrolds' essay.[12] But in George Woodcock's *The Incomparable Aphra* (1948), Mrs. Behn finally received the thorough, undistorted biography she deserved—and also a moderate amount of useful critical attention. The Platt thesis, discussed in Chapter One, led to a full-length fictional treatment, Emily Hahn's *Purple Passage* (1951), a pleasant rather than useful work which stops before Mrs. Behn began writing plays. Of the most recent accounts, Cameron's is invaluable biographically, while Henry Hargreaves' adds materially to Woodcock's criticism of the plays.[13]

Her reputation, at least among students of the period, is now fairly well settled. Hargreaves calls her "an excellent representative of minor Restoration comedy" (p. 286); Nicoll, who is bothered unnecessarily by the old "morals" issue, sums up in more negative terms: "She is no worse, and is often a great deal better, than the average playwright of her age."[14]

The present study does not present Mrs. Behn as a great writer, but as an unusually interesting and varied artist whose best comedies have not had the attention they deserve. She was not an innovator but a craftsman strongly responsive to the immediate demands of her audience. Her characters are often memorable; the methods she uses to present them she inherited or found in the works of her contemporaries. Stock types, for example, include the comical city merchant, the foolish country squire, the gallant lover, the pert young heroine, the stubborn old father or uncle, and the fashionable fop. Conflicts between these types form the structural basis of the plays; and they are used to promulgate such themes as love versus honor, youth versus age, and love versus money. Stage devices are numerous, and usually as conventional as they are successful. Disguises of all kinds abound; duels and mistakes in the dark are hardly less frequent. Most of her plays make a strong appeal to spectacle: stage directions are often elaborate; and instrumental music, masques, dances, and songs are frequently called for.

When political pressures or waning popularity ended her career as a playwright, she turned to poetry and translation. Her best songs reveal a control of rhythm, diction, and tone

rare in any period. Most of her poems and nearly all her translations, however, were topical; and they have not, therefore, out-
lived their immediate occasions. During this period she was
already ill; by the time William of Orange replaced her beloved
Stuarts on the throne, she was in dire straits and much of her
work was the product of economic necessity.

Her first novel appeared in 1684 and her first stories in 1688,
although some of the latter were clearly written earlier. In
these fourteen pieces she draws heavily on the *novella* tradition
and on French and Italian romance, not only for plot and characters but also for diction and thematic material. Her attempts
to secure verisimilitude are interesting, but she is no more important for the development of the novel than for that of the
drama. Such devices were not new; neither was an interest in
the exotic and primitive.

Despite her extensive use of conventional themes and forms,
Aphra Behn retains considerable individuality as an artist.
Specific political and social convictions, for example, find expression in nearly every work associated with her name. She is
not only a staunch Tory but personally loyal to Charles II and
James II: her dedications, political plays, panegyrics, and even
her fiction abound in praise of the noble martyr and his sons.
Her satire against the Whigs in *The Roundheads* and other
plays is the reverse of the coin; not for nothing is Sir Timothy
Treat-all a Whig or all her rovers Tories to the bone. Her
political convictions seem founded on personal loyalty and an-
tipathy to Puritanism; they were irrational and unchangeable,
not matters open to debate. The Tories are the Cavaliers, romantic and fun-loving, patrons of art and artists. Whigs in Mrs.
Behn's works are mercenary, old, treacherous, and often im-
potent.

Among her social views none is more central than her belief
that love should be free, governed neither by social convention
nor by parental command. The attempt of a parent or guardian
to force his child into an unwanted marriage is one of her most
common themes: the result of such pressure is always either
tragedy or the complete discomfiture of the parent. When the
chosen bride or groom is old, or where the match is made for

money, Mrs. Behn reacts even more strongly. The handling of this theme in *Oronooko* is typical: the old king's lust for Imoinda motivates an important segment of the action.

This attack on the common practice of the day is no mere pose. It produces some of her finest passages, and furnishes the basic situation in many of her plays and novels. It is based on an intelligent and articulate conception of what a love relationship between man and woman ought to be, a conception embodied in such lovers as Willmore and Hellena, Wittmore and Lady Fancy, Don Carlos and Julia, and Oronooko and Imoinda. Mrs. Behn is often accused of immorality because she does not inevitably associate sex with love or love with marriage; Lady Fancy, Julia, and Imoinda, for example, are already married. Such a view overlooks her insistence that marriage is merely a legalized convention made moral or immoral by the circumstances surrounding it. To Mrs. Behn, it is precisely the moral issue which is important; to many of her critics it has apparently been the legal one. If the lovers are each free to choose, are honest with each other, and are genuinely in love, then their relationship is moral whether it leads to marriage or not. If the marriage is forced on one or both parties, whether by a parent or by economic necessity, then it is not only a meaningless formality but a moral and social evil which ought to be remedied. This is the case in *Sir Patient Fancy, The False Count,* and *Oronooko.*

Nor does Mrs. Behn confuse love and lust. Miranda's attraction to the friar is lust and results in tragedy. So does the relationship between Isabella and Abdelazer. On the other hand, a relationship may be genuine and moral but not a basis for marriage—the case with Willmore and La Nuche in *The Second Part of the Rover* but not with Beaumond or Ariadne:

BEAUMOND.

'Tis morning; let's home, Ariadne, and try, if possible, to love so well to be content to marry; if we find that amendment in our hearts, to say we dare believe and trust each other, then let it be a match.

ARIADNE.

With all my heart.   (V.iii)

In short, Mrs. Behn's views may not be conventional, but they certainly must be considered moral. She embodies them in her characters and in the structure of her plays and stories, usually with technical skill and emotional power. No more can be required of any artist.

Other social attitudes are more difficult to discern. *Oronooko* has been praised as a document in the history of Negro emancipation,[15] presumably because its author treats Oronooko and Imoinda sympathetically rather than with contempt or aversion. It is not easy to decide, however, whether the choice of a Negro as hero derives from Mrs. Behn's humanitarian sympathies, her interest in the romantic and primitive, her knowledge of the popular love of the exotic, or from some combination of these factors. It is equally difficult to know, to take another example, whether her frequent use of the prostitute as a character is the result of sympathy, convention, or a desire to titillate the audience.[16] In both cases, she seems to have genuine sympathy which goes beyond other motives; but the accolades showered on her seem often tangential to her real merits and embarrassingly excessive as well.

Aphra Behn is worth reading, not because she ends or begins an era, or contributes significantly to the development of a literary genre or to the progress of an idea, but because she is an entertaining craftsman whose life and work reflect nearly every facet of a brilliant period in English literary history. She wrote successfully in every important genre except the epic, and she won the praise of most of her contemporaries and the patronage of the public. Moreover, she achieved her reputation without independent income or the advantages of birth and education; and she competed with men in a society where they had every professional advantage. It is true that most of her works do not transcend their age; if this makes her a minor artist by modern standards, it does not make her less witty, amusing, or competent. The preoccupation with major authors and the passage of nearly three centuries have left her little more than a few pages in the literary histories. But much of her best work is still fresh and meaningful, and nearly all of it is sufficiently interesting to need no apology.

Notes and References

Chapter One

1. W. J. Cameron, *New Light on Aphra Behn: An Investigation into the Facts and Fictions surrounding Her Journey to Surinam in 1663 and Her Activities as a Spy in Flanders in 1666* (University of Auckland Monograph No. 5, 1961), pp. 89-100.

2. Edmund Gosse, "Mrs. Behn," *The Athenaeum,* September 6, 1884, p. 304.

3. Montague Summers, ed., *The Works of Aphra Behn* (London and Stratford, 1915), I, xvi.

4. Victoria Sackville-West, *Aphra Behn: The Incomparable Astrea* (New York, 1928), p. 20. Summers, I, xvii, had said the column was "left blank."

5. In Walter and Clare Jerrold, *Five Queer Women* (New York, 1929).

6. A. Purvis, "Mrs. Aphra Behn," *Amateur Historian,* I, No. 9 (1953-54), inside front cover.

7. P. D. Mundy, "Aphra Behn, Novelist and Dramatist (1640?-1689)," *Notes & Queries,* CXCIX (1954), 199-201; and "Aphra Behn (1640?-1689)," *Notes & Queries,* CC (1955), 23, 456-57.

8. Ernest Bernbaum, "Mrs. Behn's Biography a Fiction," *PMLA,* XXVIII (1913), 432-53.

9. For Benjamins, see the appropriate entries in the bibliography; for Platt, see note 11 below.

10. Cameron, *op. cit.,* pp. 16-17.

11. Harrison Platt, "Astrea and Celadon: An Untouched Portrait of Aphra Behn," *PMLA,* XLIX (1934), 547.

12. The relevant parts of this letter are reprinted by Platt (see note 11 above) and may also be found in Cameron, *op. cit.,* p. 12.

13. Cameron, *op. cit.,* pp. 34-86.

14. See Henry A. Hargreaves, "Mrs. Behn's Warning of the Dutch 'Thames Plot,'" *Notes & Queries,* IX (1962), 61-63.

15. Cameron, *op. cit.,* pp. 30-32. A rather sentimental interpretation is given by Sackville-West (*op. cit.,* pp. 62-67, 75-81); a more moderate one by George Woodcock, *The Incomparable Aphra* (London and New York, 1948), pp. 35-45.

16. The second of these is reprinted by Summers, I, xxvi-xxvii, Sackville-West, *op. cit.,* pp. 77-78, and Woodcock, *op. cit.,* p. 43.

17. Emily Hahn suggests in her fanciful novel *Purple Passage* (Garden City, N. Y., 1950) that her deliverer was John Hoyle, a lawyer with whom she was apparently involved intimately later in her career. There is no evidence to support this romantic idea.

18. Henry Hargreaves, "A case for Mister Behn," *Notes & Queries,* LX (1962), 203-05.

19. Woodcock, *op. cit.,* p. 52, retells the story.

20. See Woodcock's chapter " 'The English Sappho,' " *op. cit.,* pp. 80-118, for a very thorough account, with numerous quotations from contemporary sources. The passage from Tom Brown is reprinted pp. 102-03.

21. The warrant is reprinted in Woodcock, *op. cit.,* p. 162.

22. *Ibid.,* pp. 169-70, 172.

23. This is evident from her last poems, from the "Memoirs," and from such documents as the letter accompanying her memorial poem on the death of Waller, reprinted in Woodcock, *op. cit.,* p. 194.

24. See Chapter Six.

25. This did not go unnoticed by her contemporaries. The anonymous author of *An Elegy upon the Death of Mrs. A. Behn* (1689), ends Stanza 7 with a reference to her loyalty:

> Her ever-loyal muse took no pretext
>   To discommend what once it praised;
>   And what has most her glory raised,
> Her royal master she has followed home,
> Nor would endure the world when he had lost his throne.

26. Preface to *The Younger Brother,* sig. [A5].

Chapter Two

1. Date of production from *The London Stage,* Vol. I, ed. William Van Lennep (Carbondale, 1965), 165. Compare Allardyce Nicoll, *A History of English Drama 1660-1900* (4th ed.; Cambridge, 1952), I, 390. There is often controversy about the dating of first productions of Restoration plays. Where I have found clear evidence for a given date, I have used it; otherwise I have preferred the tentative dates of *The London Stage* to those given by Nicoll or Montague Summers.

2. According to the prompter John Downes in *Roscius Anglicanus* (London, 1708), p. 34.

3. This epilogue, "By a Woman," does not appear in the first edition (1671). The reference is to Quarto 2.

4. Henry Allen Hargreaves, "The Life and Plays of Mrs. Behn" (Ph.D. dissertation, Duke University, 1961), gives considerable attention to Mrs. Behn's stagecraft in all her plays. For *The Forced Marriage*, see pp. 95-97.

5. *The London Stage*, I, 180.

6. Summers, *op. cit.*, IV, 119-20, cites Robert Davenport's *The City Night-Cap*, Greene's *Philomela*, Beaumont and Fletcher's *The Coxcomb*, and Nathaniel Field's *Amends for Ladies* as earlier analogues, and Davenport's play as a source. The *locus classicus* of the story is the tale of the Curious Impertinent in *Don Quixote*, Book IV, Chapters 6-8.

7. *The London Stage*, I, 203.

8. Compare E[dward] R[avenscroft]'s epilogue to *The Town Fop*, spoken by Sir Timothy Tawdrey:

> Observe me well, I am a man of show,
> Of noise and nonsense, as are most of you.
> Though all of you don't share with me in title,
> In character you differ very little.

9. See Pepy's diary for May 31, 1663. Floriana T. Hogan, "The Spanish Comedia and the English Comedy of Intrigue with Special Reference to Aphra Behn" (Dissertation, Boston University, 1955), argues that the Spanish *comedia* influences Mrs. Behn directly. Except in the one case of Calderon's *La Vida es Sueño*, however, she can cite little evidence. On the other hand, by Mrs. Behn's day intrigue elements were present in a good many English plays. There is no evidence that she could read Spanish, or that she knew the *comedia* in direct translation.

10. Woodcock, *op. cit.*, p. 69.

Chapter Three

1. *The London Stage*, I, 245.

2. See Henry Purcell, *Suite for String Orchestra from Abdelazer: or, The Moor's Revenge* (London, 1944); also the *Abdelazer Suite for Strings and Keyboard*, ed. E. Fandler (New York, 1947). Many songs from the plays were set to music and found their way into contemporary collections.

3. *The London Stage*, I, 249.

4. *Ibid.*, 251.

5. *Ibid.*, 256.

6. Some two hundred performances are recorded to 1775. See the appropriate volumes of *The London Stage*.

7. *The London Stage*, I, 266.

8. D. H. Miles, *The Influence of Molière on Restoration Comedy* (New York, 1910), p. 84.

9. This procedure is often defended by English critics. Dryden, for example, has Neander say in *Of Dramatic Poesy* (1668) that the "variety and copiousness" of English comic plots, "if well ordered, will afford a greater pleasure to the audience." *Of Dramatic Poesy and Other Critical Essays*, ed. George Watson (London, 1962), I, 59.

10. Although the name is given in the cast of characters as Mrs. Gwin, Summers is right in saying that the actress was Anne Quin (*op. cit.*, IV, 414). Woodcock, *op. cit.*, p. 133n., says that there is a contemporary engraving of Nell Gwyn in the role but does not give a reference.

11. *The London Stage*, I, 276, which suggests that the play may have been performed *ca.* May, 1677, under the title *The Midnight's Intrigues* (I, 249).

12. *The London Stage*, Part 2, Vol. I. John Downes wonders (*Roscius Anglicanus*, p. 227) why it did not become a repertory piece, calling it "capital fare." Henry Hargreaves ("The Life and Plays of Mrs. Aphra Behn," 165-69) defends the play, as intrigue comedy, against Allardyce Nicoll's more unreasonable strictures.

13. Summers, *op. cit.*, II, 104; Woodcock, *op. cit.*, p. 136. Nicoll, *op. cit.*, p. 391, gives *ca.* September; *The London Stage* suggests that it may have been acted as early as March (I, 281).

14. This dedication does not appear in the Harvard Library copy of the first quarto. If this is not the result of separate issues, it establishes 1696 (Quarto 2) as the earliest printing of the dedication—a date seven years after Mrs. Behn's death. It would then be necessary to consider whether Gildon had a hand in it.

15. Summers, *op. cit.*, II, 103, gives a number of analogues.

16. Emmett L. Avery, "A Tentative Calendar of Daily Theatrical Performances, 1660-1700," *Research Studies of the State College of Washington*, XIII (1945), 262, records a performance on April 4, 1680; Nicoll, *op. cit.*, 391n, thinks it likely "that the play actually was not given until April, 1681." *The London Stage* assigns it to January, 1681, on the basis of the allusion in the epilogue to the closing of Parliament, which took place January 18 (I, 293).

17. William Van Lennep, "Two Restoration Comedies," *Times Literary Supplement*, January 28, 1939, pp. 57-58, noted a Narcissus Luttrell copy which that contemporary collector had dated December 17, 1681. Since the prologue refers to the *Ignoramus*

verdict at Shaftesbury's trial on November 24, the play was probably produced between the two dates, and not in 1682 as had been thought. The discovery shifted the chronology of Mrs. Behn's play, placing *The False Count* before *The City Heiress* and probably before *The Roundheads*. George Woodcock, who apparently had not seen Van Lennep's note, adopts the reverse order.

18. See the appropriate volumes of *The London Stage*. *The Merry Counterfeit*, an afterpiece based on Mrs. Behn's play, was played at least three times in 1762, and at least once in 1771.

19. Woodcock, *op. cit.*, p. 153.

20. Summers, *op. cit.*, I, 336, gives a probable list of actors.

21. Avery, *op. cit.*, p. 263n, cites from the Bindley collection of broadsides a performance on May 15, 1682; a Luttrell copy date supports this. Nicoll, *op. cit.*, p. 391, gives *ca.* March, 1682; *The London Stage* suggests late April (I, 308).

22. Nicoll, *op. cit.*, I, 391, gives March, 1682, as the date of production; *The London Stage* agrees (I, 307).

23. *Five Love-Letters Written by a Cavalier, in Answer to the Five Love-Letters Written to Him by a Nun* (London, 1683), has been ascribed to Mrs. Behn, but on what evidence I have not been able to discover. The style is certainly unlike hers. *The Ten Pleasures of Marriage* and *The Confession of the New Married Couple, Being the Second Part . . .* (London, 1682, 1683) have been ascribed to her by John Harvey in the preface to the Navarre Society reprint (London, 1922). His ascription is based on a letter at the end of Part I signed "A. B.," but this is slim evidence indeed in the light of marked dissimilarities of style and point of view to anything else known to be by Mrs. Behn. *The London Stage*, I, 323, suggests that an alteration of Thomas Randolph's *Amyntas; or, The Impossible Dowry*, produced at some time before 1684 under the title *The Wavering Nymph; or, Mad Amyntas*, may be attributed to Mrs. Behn. As evidence, Van Lennep cites two songs in *Poems upon Several Occasions* (1684) from the play, which was apparently not printed. But since Mrs. Behn could have written the songs without having written the play, the evidence seems to me too slight to warrant the attribution.

Chapter Four

1. See note 22.
2. *The London Stage*, I, 348.
3. *Ibid.*, 356.

4. See the introduction to the edition of the play in *Ten English Farces*, ed. Leo Hughes and A. H. Scouten (Austin, Texas, 1948), and production records in the appropriate volumes of *The London Stage*.

5. The alteration is listed in the British Museum Catalogue, but I have not seen it.

6. *The London Stage*, I, 377.

7. G. Woodcock, *op. cit.*, p. 216.

8. The *London Stage*, I, 459.

9. Gerard Langbaine, *An Account of the English Dramatic Poets* . . . (Oxford, 1691), p. 529.

10. *The London Stage*, I, 254.

11. Sig. [A3]. With other plays, it is also advertised on the title page of the second edition (1697).

12. Nicoll, *op. cit.*, 440, gives *ca.* September, and notes that it has been ascribed to both Mrs. Behn and Betterton. John Genest, *Some Account of the English Stage from the Restoration in 1660 to 1830* (Bath, 1832), I, 207, says that the "original is said to have been revised by Mrs. Behn," and that she "has made some improvements, but no very material change." See *The London Stage*, I, 248, 263.

13. Henry Hargreaves calls some of the reasons for assigning *The Debauchee* to Mrs. Behn "practically incontrovertible," while *The Counterfeit Bridegroom* is "less clearly established" ("The Life and Plays of Mrs. Aphra Behn," pp. 251, 260).

14. *The London Stage*, I, 287.

15. Among other parallels, she has a pistol with which she unsuccessfully attempts to shoot Wellman (II.ii.).

16. W. Van Lennep, *op. cit.*, p. 58.

Chapter Five

1. G. Langbaine, *op. cit.*, pp. 17-18. The best discussion of sources is to be found in Hargreaves' dissertation; he collects most of the earlier material on the subject, and discusses it in detail. While I think he occasionally confuses analogues with sources, his analysis is usually sound. That of Summers is not.

2. Even here there is an echo of an earlier play. The situation between Alcippus and Erminia (II.iii) is quite close to that of Amintor and Evadne in II.i of *The Maid's Tragedy*. Also, there is always the possibility of unnoticed sources.

3. Summers, *op. cit.*, II, 102-03, gives a fairly full account of the borrowings, and of analogues. Hargreaves, "The Life and Plays of Mrs. Aphra Behn," p. 175, believes that the Calderon plot, which he says was begun in Surinam, was the basis of Mrs. Behn's play, and that the French plot was added before 1671.

4. John Wilcox, *The Relation of Molière to Restoration Comedy* (New York, 1938), pp. 146-49. Summers, *op. cit.*, IV, 4-5, is too positive about the derivation of Lady Knowell from *Les femmes savantes* and wrong in identifying Sir Credulous with M. de Pourceaugnac.

5. Miles, *op. cit.*, p. 237.

6. Montague Summers, "A Note on Mrs. Behn and a Dickens Parallel," *Notes & Queries*, CLIX (1930), 274-75. Ernst G. Matthews, who apparently had not read beyond Summers' 1915 edition, goes through the evidence again in "Montfleury's *Ecole des jaloux* and Aphra Behn's *The False Count*," *Modern Language Notes*, LIV (1939), 438-39.

7. *Op. cit.*, *pp.* 40-44. The two brief quotations which follow are from pp. 40 and 41.

8. Hughes and Scouten, *ibid.*, pp. 43-44, say that the romantic plot is "reduced to the merest thread; what is left is treated with no sign of seriousness." The first part of the statement is inaccurate; the romantic plot provides the action with a meaningful structure. Since the play is a romantic comedy insofar as the love story is concerned, it is difficult to understand why it should be seriously treated.

9. *Like Father, Like Son* is said to have been an adaptation of Randolph's *The Jealous Lovers*, but only the prologue and epilogue have survived.

10. Langbaine, *op. cit.*, p. 21.

11. Thomas Killigrew, *Comedies, and Tragedies* . . . (London, 1664), p. 439.

12. Hargreaves, "The Life and Plays of Mrs. Aphra Behn," pp. 134-35.

13. It is this fact which prompted Gerard Langbaine's remark about the eel.

14. Hargreaves, "The Life and Plays of Mrs. Aphra Behn," p. 136, agrees with Summers (*The Works of Aphra Behn*, I, 5) that the trap door episode owes something to Middleton's *Blurt, Master Constable*, IV.iii, but suggests that she "returned to the original source, 'Day 5, Novel 2, of *The Decameron*' [Genest, *op. cit.*, I, 156] for a continuation in which Blunt actually appears, 'creeping out of a Common Shore.'"

15. Hargreaves, "The Life and Plays of Mrs. Aphra Behn," pp. 136-8) argues that Hellena derives from Crispinella in Marston's *Dutch Courtesan*, and Angelica from the courtesan herself. I do not find this argument convincing, especially with reference to Hellena.

16. Including *Like Father, Like Son, The Debauchee, The Counterfeit Bridegroom,* and *The Revenge.*

Chapter Six

1. Prologue to *The City Heiress.*
2. Epilogue to *The Second Part of the Rover.*
3. Prologue to *The Lucky Chance.*
4. Prologue to *The Town Fop.*
5. It has certainly been reprinted more often than any other.
6. A few of them had appeared in *Covent Garden Drollery . . . Collected by A. B.* (London, 1672), a volume she possibly edited. See the preface to the edition of G. Thorn-Drury (London, 1928).
7. *Peri Bathous,* ed. Edna L. Steeves (New York, 1952), p. 63.
8. St. 3. The analogy between the bereaved queen and the Virgin is emphasized by the use of black letter. The Harvard Library copy has "4 April" after the date, and "2d"; it is probably a Luttrell copy.
9. The date is given from the Luttrell copy in the Houghton Library at Harvard. The poem is attributed to Mrs. Behn on the basis of Arthur Mizener's note ("Poems by Mrs. Behn," *Times Literary Supplement,* May 8, 1937, p. 364) that it is printed as hers in the 1715 edition of Buckingham's poems. It also appears in Charles Gildon's *Chorus Poetarum* (1694).
10. *A Congratulatory Poem to Her Most Sacred Majesty, on the Universal Hopes of All Loyal Persons for a Prince of Wales* (2nd ed.; London, 1688), LL. 13-19.
11. *A Congratulatory Poem to the King's Most Sacred Majesty, on the Happy Birth of the Prince of Wales* (London, 1688). The Widener Collection copy at Harvard bears Luttrell's date, June 13, 1688.
12. London, 1689. The Luttrell copy at Harvard gives the date February 26, 1689.

Chapter Seven

1. Sig. a4.
2. Pp. 112-14; 141-43 in *Poems* (1684).
3. Paul Tallemant, *Voyages de l'isle d'amour,* in *Voyages imaginaires, songes, visions, et romans cabalistiques* (Amsterdam, 1788), XXVI, 271-72.
4. Numbers 9, 20, 52, 169, and 330; pp. 303, 306, 312, 334, 367.
5. Balthasar de Bonnecorse, *La montre, second partie. Contenant la boëte, et le miroir* (Paris, 1671), p. 62.
6. Francis Barlow, *Aesop's Fables,* sig. A2.
7. Woodcock, *op. cit.,* p. 192. Montague Summers omits the work, but a few of the verses are to be found in *Selected Writings of the Ingenious Mrs. Aphra Behn* (New York, 1950), introd. by Robert Phelps.

8. Fables 22, 72, 29. See also Fables 12, 24, 30, 38, 43, 51, 68, 79, 80, 86, 90, 108.

9. Tallemant, *op. cit.*, p. 279.

10. *Abrahami Couleij angli, poemata latina* . . . (London, 1668), pp. 324-25.

Chapter Eight

1. *The Histories and Novels of the Late Ingenious Mrs. Behn* (London, 1696) included *Love-Letters: Never before Printed,* a series of exercises in the rhetoric of passion which George Woodcock and most other biographers take as genuine documents. I find this judgment questionable in the light of the popularity of epistolary fiction in the period.

2. *Love-Letters between a Nobleman and His Sister; with the History of Their Adventures,* (7th ed.; London, 1759), sig. [A6ᵛ]. Parts I and II of this edition comprise pp. 1-324; the pagination begins anew with Part III (1-253).

3. The edition I have used, for example, has "Grey's Love Letters" stamped on the spine.

4. Mrs. Behn's name does not appear on the title page, but the work is almost certainly hers. The dedication to Part III is signed "A. B." and the political ideas are typical of her Tory views.

5. Since I have been unable to examine first editions of all of the *novelle,* and since Vol. V of the Summers edition contains all Mrs. Behn's fiction except the *Love-Letters,* text references in this chapter are to page numbers of that volume except in the cases of *The Fair Jilt, Oronooko, Agnes de Castro,* and *The Lucky Mistake.* For these the references are to first editions. I have, however, checked Summers' text against later collections of the *Histories and Novels* and have normalized all quotations.

6. Summers, *The Works of Aphra Behn,* I, xlvi, n. 1.

7. Woodcock, *op. cit.*, p. 167.

8. Summers (*The Works of Aphra Behn,* V. 69) suggests that a story entitled *The Amorous Convert: Being a True Relation of What Happened in Holland* (advertised 1678) "may very well be the first sketch" of *The Fair Jilt.* This is mere conjecture, and unlikely in view of the reference to "King Charles, of blessed memory" in the middle of the story.

9. It is quite possible, however, that some events in the story may reflect her experiences in the Netherlands; cf. Cameron, *op. cit.*, pp. 18-19.

10. The advertisement on [A8ᵛ] of the first edition of *The Fair Jilt* includes the words "now in the Press, *Oronooko.*"

11. E. A. Baker, *The History of the English Novel* (London,

1929), III, 89-90. See also Wylie Sypher, "A Note on the Realism of Mrs. Behn's *Oronooko*," *Modern Language Quarterly*, III (1942), 401-5.

12. London, 1667. Ernest Bernbaum argued, in fact, that her reliance on this book was strong evidence that she had never been in Surinam. Recently, Ruthe Sheffey has suggested that the novel is indebted to *Friendly Advice to the Gentlemen-Planters of the East and West Indies* (1684) by Thomas Tryon. See her "Some Evidence for a New Source of Aphra Behn's *Oronooko*," *Studies in Philology*, LIX (1962), 52-63.

13. Rowland M. Hill, in one of the few critical articles on Mrs. Behn, notes that "the settings of *Oronooko* are, for the most part, mere background and are not used to influence directly either character or action," but calls the novel "an important link in the development of the fictional utilization of travel-book material begun by Richard Head and later made by Defoe the basis of a new fictional technique . . ." ("Aphra Behn's Use of Setting," *Modern Language Quarterly*, VII [1946], 201-2, 203).

14. Summers, *The Works of Aphra Behn*, V, 211-12, gives some analogues.

15. Woodcock, *op. cit.*, p. 207.

16. Baker (*op. cit.*, p. 85) and Woodcock (*op. cit.*, pp. 166-67) follow Summers (*The Works of Aphra Behn*, I, xlvi) in assigning this story to the 1683-84 period. I can find no basis for this date and have seen no evidence whatever to support it.

17. Woodcock, *op. cit.*, p. 198. Summers, *The Works of Aphra Behn*, I, 1, assigns this story, and also *The Unfortunate Bride*, *The Dumb Virgin*, and *The Wandering Beauty* to 1687; but he gives no reason. Baker (*op. cit.*, p. 86) follows him. Woodcock (*op. cit.*, p. 196) says the chronology is "difficult, but a rough guess at the order of their writing can be reached partly by the external evidence, such as advertisements in other publications of known date and licensings at Stationers' Hall, and partly by the steady and progressive development of an attempt at realism." He lists no such advertisements, however, and the argument from "steady and progressive development" is patently circular. Except where internal evidence strongly suggests a date of composition, I have therefore followed the order of publication throughout.

Chapter Nine

1. Gerard Langbaine, *op. cit.*, p. 17.

2. William Oldys, "Adversaria," printed in *Notes & Queries*, 2nd Series XI (1861), p. 201.

3. In a letter to Elizabeth Thomas, written in 1699, Dryden cautions her to avoid "the license which Mrs. Behn allowed herself, of writing loosely, and giving . . . some scandal to the modesty of her sex." *The Letters of John Dryden,* ed. Charles E. Ward (Durham, N. C., 1942), p. 127.

4. John Doran, *"Their Majesties' Servants,"* Annals of the English Stage . . . (London, 1888), I, 239.

5. *Two Centuries of Testimony in Favor of Mrs. Aphra Behn . . .* (London, 1872).

6. "Literary Garbage," *Saturday Review,* XXXIII (January 27, 1872), 109.

7. *Athenaeum,* March 16, 1872, p. 303.

8. In her essay on Aphra Behn for the "English Women of Letters Series" (London, 1863).

9. Paul Siegel, "Aphra Behn's Gedichte und Prosawerke," *Anglia,* XXV (1902), 86-128; 329-85.

10. Paul Elmer More, "A Bluestocking of the Restoration," *The Nation,* CIII (1916), 299-302; 322-23.

11. E. A. Baker, ed., *The Novels of Mrs. Aphra Behn* (London and New York, 1905), in the "Library of Early Novelists" series.

12. In Walter and Clare Jerrold's *Five Queer Women.*

13. Cameron's book is discussed in Chapter One; Hargreaves' dissertation is discussed throughout the chapters on Mrs. Behn's plays. In addition, Ruthe T. Sheffey has surveyed "The Literary Reputation of Aphra Behn" in a University of Pennsylvania dissertation (1959), and Alfred Leja has studied her politics in "Aphra Behn—Tory," a dissertation done at the University of Texas in 1962.

14. Nicoll, *op. cit.,* p. 221.

15. Edwin D. Johnson, "Aphra Behn's *Oronooko," Journal of Negro History,* X (1925), 334-42.

16. Hargreaves ("The Life and Plays of Mrs. Aphra Behn," pp. 286 ff.), suggests that she presents courtesans with unusual sympathy, and notes that her "bad" characters usually have some good traits.

Selected Bibliography

PRIMARY SOURCES

The Histories and Novels of the Late Ingenious Mrs. Behn. London: for S. Briscoe, 1696. Subsequent editions add and subtract material.

Histories, Novels, and Translations, Written by the Most Ingenious Mrs. Behn: The Second Volume. London: for S. B., 1700.

Plays Written by the Late Ingenious Mrs. Behn. 2 vols. London: for J. Tonson and R. Wellington, 1702.

————. 2nd ed. 4 vols. London: for M. W., 1716. Includes eight additional plays.

————. 3rd ed. 4 vols. London: for M. Poulson, 1724. Includes *The Younger Brother.*

Poems by Eminent Ladies. Vol. I. London: for R. Baldwin, 1755. A selection from Mrs. Behn's poetry is given on pp. 59-170.

The Plays, Histories, and Novels of the Ingenious Mrs. Aphra Behn. 6 vols. London: Pearson, 1871. A reprint of the 1724 *Plays* and of the 1751 ed. of the *Histories and Novels.*

The Novels of Mrs. Aphra Behn, introd. by ERNEST A. BAKER. London: Routledge, 1913. Includes only those stories in the 1698 ed. of the *Histories and Novels.*

The Works of Aphra Behn, ed. MONTAGUE SUMMERS. 6 vols. London: Heinemann, 1915. The only modern edition, but incomplete and erratically edited.

Ten English Farces, ed. LEO HUGHES and A. H. SCOUTEN. Austin, Texas: University of Texas Press, 1948. Includes *The Emperor of the Moon.*

Selected Writings of the Ingenious Mrs. Aphra Behn, introd. by ROBERT PHELPS. New York: Grove Press, 1950. Includes *The Dutch Lover,* four stories, and selected poems.

The Rover, ed. FREDERICK M. LINK. Lincoln: University of Nebraska Press, 1967. Includes a critical discussion of the play.

SECONDARY SOURCES

ALLEMAN, GELLERT S. *Matrimonial Law and the Materials of Restoration Comedy.* Philadelphia, n. p., 1942. Useful for understanding the relation between contemporary law and the resolution of love plots in the comedies.

AVERY, EMMETT L. "A Tentative Calendar of Daily Theatrical Performances, 1660-1770," *Research Studies of the State College of Washington,* XIII (1945), 225-83. Records known production dates of plays.

BAKER, DAVID E., ISAAC REED, and STEPHEN JONES. *Biographia Dramatica; or, A Companion to the Playhouse.* 2 vols. London: for Rivington & others, 1782. Brief; useful only as an early account of Mrs. Behn.

BAKER, ERNEST A. *The History of the English Novel.* Vol. III. London: Witherby, 1924-39. A standard account of Mrs. Behn's fiction.

BAKER, HERSCHEL. "Mrs. Behn Forgets," *Studies in English* (Austin: University of Texas Publication 4226, 1942), pp. 121-23. Calls attention to the omission of the phrase "especially of our sex" in some copies of *The Rover.*

BENJAMINS, H. D. "Een Koninklijke Slaav in Suriname," *De West-Indische Gids,* I (October, 1919), 474-77.

———. "Is Aphra Behn in Suriname Geweest?" *De West-Indische Gids,* VIII (February, 1927), 451-62.

———. "Nog Eens: Aphra Behn," *De West-Indische Gids,* II (February, 1921), 517-38. The three articles constitute an early and fairly thorough discussion of the evidence for Mrs. Behn's presence in Surinam. Used extensively by Victoria Sackville-West in her book.

BERNBAUM, ERNEST. *The Drama of Sensibility.* Cambridge: Harvard University Press, 1925. Argues that several of Mrs. Behn's plays are precursors of the type, largely because of their treatment of love and marriage.

———. "Mrs. Behn's Biography a Fiction," *Publications of the Modern Language Association,* XXVIII (1913), 432-53.

———. "Mrs. Behn's *Oronooko,*" *Anniversary Papers by Colleagues and Pupils of George Lyman Kittredge* (Boston: Ginn, 1913), pp. 419-35. These two articles, now largely discredited, present the argument that Mrs. Behn was never in Surinam.

BOSWELL, ELEANORE. *The Restoration Court Stage.* Cambridge: Harvard University Press, 1932. Useful for understanding the way Mrs. Behn's plays were staged.

CAMERON, WILLIAM J. *New Light on Aphra Behn.* Auckland: University of Auckland Press, 1961. The best study of Mrs. Behn's career as a spy and of the Surinam question.

CIBBER, COLLEY. *An Apology.* . . . London: for the author, 1740. Useful for minor details about the plays.

DOBREE, BONAMY, *Restoration Comedy: 1660-1720*. Oxford: Clarendon Press, 1924. A standard work; not very good on Aphra Behn.

DOWNES, JOHN. *Roscius Anglicanus*. London: n. p., 1708. Useful details about the plays.

FAIRCHILD, HOXIE N. *The Noble Savage*. New York: Columbia University Press, 1928. An important study of the tradition to which *Oronooko* is often assigned.

FUJIMURA, THOMAS H. *The Restoration Comedy of Wit*. Princeton: Princeton University Press, 1952. Important study of a kind of comedy represented in such plays as *The Rover*.

GENEST, JOHN. *Some Account of the English Stage from . . . 1660-1830*. 10 vols. Bath: by H. E. Carrington, 1832. An important nineteenth-century history.

GOSSE, EDMUND. "Mrs. Behn," *Athenaeum*, II (1884), 304. An announcement of the author's discovery of Mrs. Behn's "identity." Erroneous but very influential.

HAHN, EMILY. *Purple Passage: A Novel about a Lady both Famous and Fantastic*. Garden City, N. Y.: Doubleday, 1950. A fanciful account of Mrs. Behn's early career, based on Harrison Platt's theory.

HAMELIUS, PAUL. "The Source of Southerne's *Fatal Marriage*," *Modern Language Review*, IV (1909), 352-56. Points out Southerne's debt to *The History of the Nun*.

HARBAGE, ALFRED. *Thomas Killigrew, Cavalier Dramatist*. Philadelphia: University of Pennsylvania Press, 1930. Useful for its account of Killigrew's *Thomaso*, on which *The Rover* was based.

HARGREAVES, HENRY A. "A Case for Mr. Behn," *Notes & Queries*, IX (1962), 203-05. Suggests that one "Joachim Beene, Hamburgher," mentioned in the *Calendar of State Papers*, may be Mrs. Behn's husband.

——. "The Life and Plays of Mrs. Aphra Behn." Ph.D. dissertation, Duke University, 1961. The best and most scholarly study of Mrs. Behn's plays; Chapter One is an excellent summary of the biographical materials up to 1960.

——. "Mrs. Behn's Warning of the Dutch 'Thames Plot,'" *Notes & Queries*, IX (1962), 61-63. Argues, against Bernbaum, that Mrs. Behn did give advance warning of a Dutch plan to sink ships in the Thames.

HERRICK, MARVIN T. *Tragicomedy: Its Origin and Development in Italy, France, and England*. Urbana: University of Illinois Press, 1955. Helpful in understanding Mrs. Behn's early plays.

HILL, ROWLAND M. "Aphra Behn's Use of Setting," *Modern Lan-*

guage Quarterly, VII (1946), 189-203. A useful study of one aspect of Mrs. Behn's fiction.

HOGAN, FLORIANA T. "The Spanish Comedia and the English Comedy of Intrigue with Special Reference to Aphra Behn." Ph.D. dissertation, Boston University, 1955. Argues, without adequate evidence, that Mrs. Behn's intrigue plays are directly influenced by the Spanish *comedia.*

HOTSON, LESLIE. *The Commonwealth and Restoration Stage.* Cambridge: Harvard University Press, 1928. Helpful in understanding the mechanics of stage production of the plays.

HUDSON, WILLIAM H. "Two Novelists of the English Restoration." *Idle Hours in a Library.* San Francisco: W. Doxey, 1897. An appreciation.

HUGHES, LEO. *A Century of English Farce.* Princeton: Princeton University Press, 1956. A good discussion of the tradition to which *The Emperor of the Moon* and *The False Count* belong.

JACOB, GILES. *The Poetical Register.* 2 vols. London: Curll, 1719-20. Early, brief comment.

JERROLD, WALTER and CLARE. *Five Queer Women.* New York: Brentano, 1929. The essay on Mrs. Behn is important for introducing new details relating to her early career.

KRUTCH, JOSEPH W. *Comedy and Conscience after the Restoration.* 2nd ed. New York: Columbia University Press, 1949. Helpful in understanding the dramatic tradition of which Mrs. Behn was a part.

LANGBAINE, GERARD. *An Account of the English Dramatic Poets.* Oxford: for G. West and H. Clements, 1691. One of the earliest accounts; brief, but useful for its remarks on the sources and reception of the plays.

———. *The Lives and Characters of the English Dramatic Poets,* ed. CHARLES GILDON. London: for T. Leigh and W. Turner, 1699. Particularly concerned with sources; a revision of the above.

LEJA, ALFRED E. "Aphra Behn—Tory." Ph.D. dissertation, University of Texas, 1962. The only full study of Mrs. Behn's politics. Very useful.

"Literary Garbage," *Saturday Review,* XXXIII (January 27, 1872), 109-10. An anonymous bluenose attack on Pearson's reprint of 1871.

The London Stage, 1660-1800, ed. EMMETT L. AVERY, A. H. SCOUTEN, and GEORGE W. STONE. 8 vols. Carbondale: Southern Illinois University Press, 1960-65. The best modern source for information about the production, popularity, and casts of the plays.

LYNCH, JAMES J. *Box, Pit, and Gallery.* Berkeley: University of California Press, 1953. Useful background study.

[174]

Selected Bibliography

MANDACH, ANDRÉ DE. *Molière et la comédie le moeurs en Angleterre (1606-68): Essai de littérature comparée.* Neuchatel: A. et W. Seiler, 1945. Studies the influence of Molière on Restoration comedy.

"Memorials of Literary Characters.—No. XIV," *Gentleman's Magazine,* n.s. I (1836), 481-82. Prints some letters of Mrs. Behn for the first time.

MIGNON, ELIZABETH. *Crabbed Age and Youth: The Old Men and Women in the Restoration Comedy of Manners.* Durham: Duke University Press, 1946. A useful background study of one kind of stock character.

MILES, DUDLEY H. *The Influence of Molière on Restoration Comedy.* New York: Columbia University Press, 1910. Useful for studying Mrs. Behn's use of Molière.

MIZENER, ARTHUR. "Poems by Mrs. Behn," *Times Literary Supplement,* May 8, 1937, p. 364. Tracks a few poems in the maze of miscellanies published in the period.

MORE, PAUL E. "A Bluestocking of the Restoration," *The Nation,* CIII (1916), 299-302, 322-23. A depreciation.

MUNDY, P. D. "Aphra Behn (1640?-1689)," *Notes & Queries,* CC (1955), 23, 456-57. Attempts to track Mrs. Behn's ancestry among the Amis and Bean families of Elmsted and Etham.

NICOLL, ALLARDYCE. *A History of English Drama, 1660-1900.* Rev. ed. Vol I. Cambridge: Cambridge University Press, 1952. Useful as a general historical account, of little importance critically.

NOYES, ROBERT GAYLE. "Conventions of Song in Restoration Traggedy," *PMLA,* LIII (1938), 162-88. Useful for understanding the function of lyrics in *Abdelazer.*

OLDYS, WILLIAM. From MS "Adversaria," *Notes & Queries,* 2 Ser. XI (1861), 201-02. Brief remarks on Mrs. Behn.

PLATT, HARRISON G., JR. "Astrea and Celadon: An Untouched Portrait of Aphra Behn," *PMLA,* XLIX (1934), 544-59. An important biographical study. Platt refutes Bernbaum, and links Mrs. Behn's presence in and departure from Surinam with William Scot.

PURVIS, A. "Mrs. Aphra Behn," *Amateur Historian,* I, No. 9 (1953-54), inside front cover, opp. p. 261. This article overturned Gosse's account of Aphra Amis, standard since 1884.

RAMSARAN, J. A. "*Oronooko:* A Study of the Factual Elements," *Notes & Queries,* VII (1960), 142-45. One of the numerous articles which help to refute Bernbaum's papers.

SACKVILLE-WEST, VICTORIA. *Aphra Behn: The Incomparable Astrea.* New York: Viking, 1928. An impressionistic and sympathetic account limited largely to Mrs. Behn's early career.

SEEBER, EDWARD D. "Oronooko and Crusoe's Man Friday," *Modern Language Quarterly*, XII (1951), 286-91. Suggests that Friday is modeled on Oronooko.

———. "*Oronooko* in France in the XVIIIth Century," *PMLA*, LI (1936), 953-59. Interesting study of the influence of Mrs. Behn's hero.

SHEFFEY, RUTHE T. "The Literary Reputation of Aphra Behn." Ph.D. dissertation, University of Pennsylvania, 1959. Traces the reputation of Mrs. Behn from her own lifetime to the mid-twentieth century.

———. "Some Evidence for a New Source of Aphra Behn's *Oronooko*," *Studies in Philology*, LIX (1962), 52-63. Suggests Thomas Tryon's *Friendly Advice to the Gentlemen-Planters of the East and West Indies* (1684).

SHERBO, ARTHUR. *English Sentimental Drama*. East Lansing: Michigan State University, 1957. Good background study.

SHUSTER, GEORGE N. *The English Ode from Milton to Keats*. New York: Columbia University Press, 1940. Useful in understanding Mrs. Behn's use of the pindaric ode in her occasional verse.

SIEGEL, PAUL. "Aphra Behn's Gedichte und Prosawerke," *Anglia*, XXV (1902), 86-128, 329-85. The only significant account of Mrs. Behn in German.

SMITH, JOHN H. *The Gay Couple in Restoration Comedy*. Cambridge: Harvard University Press, 1948. Provides background for understanding Mrs. Behn's many pairs of lovers.

SOUTHERN, RICHARD. *Changeable Scenery: Its Origin and Development in the British Theatre*. London: Faber, 1952. Helpful in understanding Mrs. Behn's interest in and use of stage effects.

SPRAGUE, ARTHUR C. *Beaumont and Fletcher on the Restoration Stage*. Cambridge: Harvard University Press, 1926. A general study which provides background for understanding Mrs. Behn's early plays.

SUMMERS, MONTAGUE. "A Note on Mrs. Behn and a Dickens Parallel," *Notes & Queries*, CLIX (1930), 274-75. Shows the influence of Montfleury's *Ecole des Jaloux* (1664) on the main plot of *The False Count*.

TUCKER, JOSEPH E. "The Earliest English Translation of La Rochefoucauld's *Maximes*," *Modern Language Notes*, LXIV (1949), 413-15. Earlier writers, including Woodcock, had put Mrs. Behn's translation first; Tucker properly credits John Davies of Kidwelly (1670).

Two Centuries of Testimony in Favour of Mrs. Aphra Behn. . . . London: Pearson, 1872. Pearson here reprints earlier praise of Mrs. Behn in defense of his reprint of her works (1871).

[176]

Selected Bibliography

Van Lennep, William. "Two Restoration Comedies," *Times Literary Supplement*, January 28, 1939, pp. 57-58. Gives information about two Luttrell copies which help date the production of *The False Count* and *The Revenge*.

Vernon, P. F. "Marriage of Convenience and the Moral Code of Restoration Comedy," *Essays in Criticism*, XII (1962), 370-87. Useful study of a theme which interested Mrs. Behn.

Wagenknecht, Edward C. "In Praise of Mrs. Behn," *Colophon*, Part XVIII (1934). An appreciation, very well written.

Wilcox, John. *The Relation of Molière to Restoration Comedy*. New York: Columbia University Press, 1938. Helpful in understanding the English use of Molière; relevant especially to *Sir Patient Fancy* and *The False Count*.

Wilson, John H. *The Influence of Beaumont and Fletcher on Restoration Drama*. Columbus: Ohio State University Press, 1928. Discusses the tradition evident in Mrs. Behn's early plays.

Woodcock, George. *The Incomparable Aphra*. London: Boardman, 1948. The only good full-length introduction to Mrs. Behn's life and works. Rather more biographical than critical, but readable and fairly accurate except for dates. Very good in establishing the context of her life.

Index

Abdelazer, 23, *41-44,* 52, 95, 96, 97, 103, 108
"The Adventure of the Black Lady," 147
Aesop's Fables, 122, 123
Agnes de Castro, 123, *142-143,* 144, 145
The Amorous Prince, 22, 24, 33-35, 60, 62, 92, 93, 105
The Amours of Philander and Sylvia, 132
Arlequin empereur dans la lune, 78, 95
Arlington, Henry Bennet, Earl of, 21
Arundel, Henry Howard, Earl of, 26

Bacon, Nathaniel, 80, 81, 82, 92
Baker, David E., 90
Baker, Ernest A., 141, 149, 153
Barlow, Francis, 121
Barry, Elizabeth, 44, 52, 58, 65, 73, 77
Beaumont, Francis, and John Fletcher, 29, 38, 60, 92
Benjamins, H. D., 19
Bernbaum, Ernest, 19, 21
Betterton, Thomas, 22, 33, 43, 52, 55, 58, 73, 77, 88, 90, 105
Betterton, Mrs. Thomas, 22, 33, 43, 52, 55
Blake, William, 119, 153

Bonnecorse, Balthasar de, 27, 121
Bracegirdle, Anne, 52, 82
Brémond, Sébastien, 83, 92
Brillac, Mlle de, 142
Brome, Richard, 85, 86, 87, 94, 101
Brown, Thomas, 23
Buckingham, George Villiers, 2nd Duke of, 25, 121
Bunyan, John, 142
Burnet, Gilbert, 28, 114
Butler, Charlotte, 73
Byam, William, 19, 20

Calderon de la Barca, 61, 93
Cameron, William J., 17, 19-20, 21, 154
"Cease, Cease, Aminta to Complain," 109
Cervantes, Miguel de, 93
Charles II, 21, 24, 25, 26, 27, 68, 69, 105, 106, 112, 114, 123, 135, 136, 155
Cibber, Theophilus, 152
The City Heiress, 24, 26, *69-73,* 92, 94, 95, 101, 106, 108
Cleve, C., 128
Cockburn, Catherine, 152
Committee of Safety, 26, 100
"A Congratulatory Poem to . . . Queen Mary," 114
Congreve, William, 24, 31, 51, 71, 148

The Conquest of Granada, 43

The Counterfeit Bridegroom, 85, 86-87, 88

"The Court of the King of Bantam," 135-136

Cowley, Abraham, 27, 102, 116, 127, 128, 129

Cowley, Hannah, 77

Creech, Thomas, 23, 110

Cromwell, Mrs. Oliver, 100

Crowne, John, 25

Currer, Elizabeth, 55, 58, 65, 68, 73, 87, 103

Davenant, William, 22

Davenport, Robert, 93

The Debauchee, 85-86, 87, 88

Defoe, Daniel, 138, 139, 142

Desborough, Lady Jane, 100

Dibden, Charles, 152

"The Disappointment," 109

A Discovery of New Worlds, 124-125

Doran, John, 152, 153

Dorset, Charles Sackville, 6th Earl of, 111

Downes, John, 22, 56

Dryden, John, 22, 23, 24, 25, 27, 37, 43, 44, 79, 101, 105, 106, 116, 123, 153

Duckenfield, Robert, 68

The Duke of Guise, 25, 27

The Dumb Virgin, 148-149

D'Urfey, Thomas, 25, 83, 92

The Dutch Lover, 22, 23, 35-40, 41, 92, 108

The Emperor of the Moon, 27, 77-80, 92, 95, 103, 152

Etherege, George, 22, 24

Exclusion Bill, 26, 68

The Fair Jilt, 137-139, 143, 145

The False Count, 24, 25, 66-68, 78, 92, 94, 101, 156

"A Farewell to Celadon," 110

Fatouville, Nolant de, 95

The Feigned Courtesans, 24, 56-58, 63, 77, 91, 103

Fielding, Henry, 142, 150

Fleetwood, Charles, 26, 68

Fontenelle, Bernard le Bovier de, 27, 124

The Forced Marriage, 22, 24, 29-33, 34, 35, 48, 60, 62, 91, 105, 107

Ford, John, 38, 92

Genest, John, 87, 88, 152

Gildon, Charles, 17, 28, 82, 83, 84, 109

"The Golden Age," 110-111

Gosse, Edmund, 17, 18, 60

Grafton, Henry Fitzroy, 1st Duke of, 26

Grey, Forde, 130, 132, 133

Guilleragues, Gabriel, Count de, 130, 144, 146, 147

Gwyn, Nell, 56

Hahn, Emily, 21, 154

Hargreaves, Henry A., 21, 35, 51, 59, 71, 85, 86, 88, 154

Harley, Sir Robert, 20

Hewson, John, 68, 104

Histories and Novels, 17, 135, 146, 147

The History of Don Fenise, 38, 92

The History of Oracles, 124

The History of the Nun, 143-145, 148

Hoyle, John, 23, 110

Hughes, Leo, 95

James II, 24, 25, 27, 58, 65, 112, 115, 155
Jenkins, George, 80, 82
Jerrold, Walter and Clare, 18, 154
Jevon, Thomas, 77, 80
Jonson, Ben, 37, 101

Kavanagh, Julia, 153
Kemble, John Philip, 52
Killigrew, Thomas, 21, 22, 48, 62, 97, 98, 99, 100, 101

La Calprenède, Gauthier de Costes, Seigneur de, 60, 92
Lambert, John, 26, 68
Lambert, Lady Frances, 68, 69, 100
Langbaine, Gerard, 17, 85, 88, 90, 91, 92, 97, 101, 152
Lansdowne, George Granville, Lord, 23
La Rochenfoucauld, François, Duc de, 27, 120
Lee, John, 68, 73
Lee, Nathaniel, 22, 25
Leigh, Anthony, 55, 58, 77, 80
L'Estrange, Roger, 114, 147
"A Letter to a Brother of the Pen," 109
Like Father, Like Son, 73
Lilly, William, 100
The London Cuckolds, 135
The London Stage, 48
Loveday, Robert, 92
"Love in Fantastic Triumph Sat," 42, 108
Love Letters from a Nobleman to His Sister, 130-135
Love Letters of a Nun to a Cavalier, 144
The Lover's Watch, 121

The Lucky Chance, 23, 27, 56, 74-77, 90, 91
The Lucky Mistake, 145-146
Lust's Dominion, 41, 96, 97
Luttrell, Narcissus, 90
Lycidus, 109, 111, 120, *126-127*

Marston, John, 88, 89
Martin, Colonel George, 19, 83
Massinger, Philip, 70, 94, 101
"Memoirs on the Life of Mrs. Behn," 17, 18-19, 28
Middleton, Thomas, 70, 87, 94, 101
Miles, D. H., 53, 93
Miscellany, Being a Collection of Poems, 109, 111, 120
"A Miscellany of New Poems," 109
Molière, 52, 53, 54, 67, 93, 94, 101
Monck, George, 68
Monmouth, Duke of, 25, 26, 27, 68, 130, 131, 133
Montfleury, A., 66, 68, 94
More, Paul Elmer, 153
Mountford, Will, 52
Mulgrave, John Sheffield, 3rd Earl of, 120
Mundy, P. D., 18

Nicoll, Allardyce, 154
Nokes, James, 55, 58, 65, 68, 73, 77
"The Nun, or Perjured Beauty," *146-147,* 148

Oates, Titus, 25, 26, 56, 68, 104, 107, 123
"Of Trees," 128-129
Oldfield, Ann, 52
The Old Pretender, 113, 114

Oldys, William, 152
"On a Juniper Tree," 109
"On Desire," 111
"On Mr. J. H.," 110
"On . . . Sir Francis Fane," 111
"On the Author of . . . *The Way to Health*," 111
"On the Death of Mr. Grinhill," 110
"On the Death of the Late Earl of Rochester," 111
Oronooko, 19, 20, 28, 80, 83, 110, *139-142*, 143, 145, 151, 153, 156, 157
Otway, Thomas, 22, 23, 25, 26, 44
"Our Cabal," 108, 109
Ovid, 116
Ovid's Epistles, 116

Pain, Henry, 138
"A Paraphrase on Oenone to Paris," 116
"A Pastoral Pindaric," 111
"A Pastoral to Mr. Stafford," 111
Pearson, John, 153
Pepys, Samuel, 39
Peri Bathous, 110
Philips, Katherine, 21, 152
A Pindaric on the Death of Our Late Sovereign, 112
A Pindaric Poem on . . . James II, 112
"A Pindaric to Mr. P," 111
Pinkethman, William, 80
Platt, Harrison, 19, 20, 154
Poems (1684), 27, 108, 117, 118
A Poem . . . to . . . Catherine Queen Dowager, 112
Pope, Alexander, 102, 152, 153
Prior, Matthew, 107

Purcell, Henry, 43
Purvis, A., 18

Quin, Anne, 52, 55

Randolph, Thomas, 73
Ravenscroft, Edward, 22, 23
The Revenge, 85, *88-90*
Richardson, Samuel, 31, 135, 142
Rochester, John Wilmot, 2nd Earl of, 120
Romulus & Hersilia, 27
Roscommon, Wentworth Dillon, 4th Earl of, 125
Rotrou, Jean, 53
The Roundheads, 24, 26, *68-69*, 73, 95 100, 101, 104, 155
Rousseau, J. J., 141
The Rover (I), 24, *48-52*, 55, 56, 57, 63, 65, 70, 72, 86, 87, 89, 95, 97, 98, 99, 105, 120, 152
The Rover (II), 24, 25, *62-66*, 69, 78, 90, 95, 97, 99, 103, 105, 108, 156
The Rye House Plot, 130, 136

Sackville-West, Victoria, 18, 153-154
Sandford, Samuel, 82
Scarron, Paul, 53, 135
Scot, Thomas, 20
Scot, William, 20
Scouten, A. H., 95
Seneca Unmasqued, 120
Settle, Elkanah, 22
Shadwell, Thomas, 22, 37
Shaftesbury, Anthony Ashley Cooper, 1st Earl of, 25, 26, 68, 70, 104, 123
Shakespeare, William, 37, 79, 82, 101, 145

Index

Shelley, Mary, 141
Sheridan, Thomas B., 54
Shirley, James, 91, 101
Siegel, Paul, 153
Sir Patient Fancy, 24, 52-56, 57, 92, 93, 101, 105, 108, 156
Slingsby, Mary Lee, Lady, 27
Smith, Ned, 52, 55, 58, 65, 68
Southerne, Thomas, 152
The Spectator, 77
Strange News from Virginia, 80, 92
Summers, Montague, 18, 58, 59, 60, 62, 85, 88, 94, 139, 153
Swinburne Algernon, 119, 153

Tallemant, Abbé Paul, 27, 118, 120, 126, 127
Tate, Nahum, 128
Tatham, John, 68, 100
Tennyson, Alfred, Lord, 144
Thackeray, William M., 84
Three Histories, 143
"To . . . Christopher Duke of Albermarle," 113
"To Mr. Creech," 110
"To Mrs. W," 110
Tonson, Jacob, 116
"To the Honorable Edward Howard," 110
Tonson, Jacob, 116
"To the Memory of . . . George Duke of Buckingham," 113
The Town Fop, 24, 44-48, 67, 90, 95, 108

Trefry, John, 19
Tuke, Sir Samuel, 39

Underhill, Cave, 52, 58, 65, 68, 80, 82
The Unfortunate Bride, 148
"The Unfortunate Happy Lady," *136-137*, 150
The Unhappy Mistake, 149-151

Van Dale, Antonius, 124
Van Lennep, William, 90
A Voyage to the Island of Love, 108, 118, 119, 121, 124, 126

The Wandering Beauty, 147-148
Warren, George, 19, 141
"When Jemmy First Began to Love," 108-109
The Widow Ranter, 80-82, 83, 84, 90, 92
Wilkes, Thomas, 152
Wilkins, George, 44, 95, 96, 136
William III, 155
Woffington, Peg, 52
The Woman Turned Bully, 85
Woodcock, George, 18, 21, 22, 23, 27, 40, 58, 59, 69, 82, 85, 122, 137, 149, 154
Wycherley, William, 22, 24, 71

Young, Edward, 97
The Younger Brother, 17, 77, 82-84, 91
The Young King, 24, 58-62, 92, 101, 104, **105**